To Heal a Broken Life

The Art of Overcoming

Claude Miragliotta

Order this book online at www.trafford.com/06-3038
or email orders@trafford.com

Most Trafford titles are also available at major online book retailers.

Note for Librarians: A cataloguing record for this book is available from Library and Archives Canada at www.collectionscanada.ca/amicus/index-e.html

ISBN: 978-1-4251-1279-0

We at Trafford believe that it is the responsibility of us all, as both individuals and corporations, to make choices that are environmentally and socially sound. You, in turn, are supporting this responsible conduct each time you purchase a Trafford book, or make use of our publishing services. To find out how you are helping, please visit www.trafford.com/responsiblepublishing.html

Our mission is to efficiently provide the world's finest, most comprehensive book publishing service, enabling every author to experience success. To find out how to publish your book, your way, and have it available worldwide, visit us online at www.trafford.com/10510

www.trafford.com

North America & international
toll-free: 1 888 232 4444 (USA & Canada)
phone: 250 383 6864 ♦ fax: 250 383 6804
email: info@trafford.com

The United Kingdom & Europe
phone: +44 (0)1865 722 113 ♦ local rate: 0845 230 9601
facsimile: +44 (0)1865 722 868 ♦ email: info.uk@trafford.com

10 9 8 7 6 5 4 3 2

To my father, Alphonse,
the lobster fisherman
who
secretly wanted to be a singer.

Contents

Acknowledgments

WRITING THIS BOOK has been a journey of inspiration, excitement and hard work. It is also something I knew I should be doing—something I felt I was meant to do.

This passage of writing is the kind of adventure the nine-year-old boy in me had longed to embark on. It is the result of what I have been through and it has led to the type of life I've now chosen to live. To choose one's direction in life is wonderful, rather than heading in the direction we think society expects us to follow.

I am thankful to life for all the difficult years, for all the twists and turns. It was only because of my stubborn resistance to change that it took me so long to heed the message and head in the direction it was guiding me towards all along.

To Maggie Rourke, my English teacher during adult literacy classes 17 years ago: you came to me so excited about an assignment I had written, and said, 'You must write'. You stirred the distant memory in me of the little boy who sought adventure.

To Andrew Burke, who stood up during one of his creative writing classes and said, 'There's only one person here who is going to be a writer'—and then named me. I was the least educated in the group and struggled to complete five sentences during our speed writing sessions when everyone else turned out one or two pages. You gave me confidence when I needed it.

Jennifer Marr, of The Inspiration Factory, whose books and audio products greatly inspired me along the way: your suggestion for me to write about my experience left me thinking that maybe I could—and eventually I did.

To my darling Zita: thank you for all your early proofreading. You told me my writing was inspiring when I thought it might be rubbish. Your unfailing support and love is a gift that I'm grateful for each day. It is such a joy to be in your company.

Adrian Glamorgan: you always encouraged and advised me as a teacher and then as a friend.

Steve Henderson, a good friend and fellow student: you believed in me when I doubted myself.

To Deb Fitzpatrick of ProofEd Editing Services for the substantive edit and all the following edits: you were a pleasure to work with. Thank you for not trying to change my style and for the wonderful work that you've done. Your editing has ensured that my book is better than it otherwise would have been. Thanks also to Genevieve Hawks for her work on the final proofread. My gratitude to Georgia Richter for her concluding edits and proofread: your fresh eyes and experience helped reduce those errors that so often sneak past us.

To Des McKenzie of Gateway Printing: thanks for a great cover. You went out of your way to help at every turn.

To Jay of Jay Heifetz Photography: it's a wonderful photo. You finally got me to smile (it must have been your joke).

My thanks to Trafford Publishing, from the receptionist right through to the technicians. Everyone at Trafford has gone out of their way to be helpful, friendly and supportive. Your experience in the self-publishing field and your support of authors has been a real benefit and greatly encouraging.

I would like to thank the following authors whose work not only assisted my healing but also inspired me along the way:

Jake Bernstein 2003, *No Bull Investing,* Dearborn Trade Publishing, USA.

Jack Canfield & Mark Victor Hansen 1995, *The Best of the Original Chicken Soup for the Soul,* (audio), HCI Audio Book, Deerfield Beach, Florida.

—— 2000 *Chicken Soup for the Writer's Soul,* Health Communications Inc, Deerfield Beach, Florida.

Paulo Coelho 1993, *The Alchemist,* Harper Collins, New York.

His Holiness the Dalai Lama 2000, *The Little Book Of Wisdom,* Rider, London.

—— & Howard C. Cutler, MD 1998, *The Art of Happiness—A Handbook For Living*, Hodder, Sydney.

Dr John F. Demartini 2004, *How To Make One Hell Of A Profit And Still Get To Heaven,* Hay House Australia Pty Ltd, Alexandria, NSW.

Dr Wayne W. Dyer 1992, *Real Magic,* HarperCollins, Sydney.

—— 2001, *There's a Spiritual Solution to Every Problem,* (audio), HarperCollins Publishers Inc, USA.

Shakti Gawain 2002, *Creative Visualization,* Nataraj Publishing, Novato, California.

John Gray 1993, *Men Are From Mars—Women Are From Venus,* Thorsons, London.

Louise L. Hay 1991, *The Power is Within You*, Specialist Publications, Concord, Australia.

—— 1988, *You Can Heal Your Life*, Specialist Publications, Concord, Australia.

Harville Hendrix 1995, *Finding Love,* (audio), Sounds True, Boulder, Colorado.

Napoleon Hill 1987, *Think & Grow Rich,* (audio), Napoleon Hill Foundation, USA.

Robert T. Kiyosaki 1997, *Rich Dad Poor Dad*, TechPress Inc, Arizona, USA.

—— 1998, *Cashflow Quadrant*, TechPress Inc, Arizona, USA.

Dr Norman Vincent Peale 1986, *The Power Of Positive Thinking,* (audio), Sound Ideas, New York.

Dr John Sarno 1991, *Healing Back Pain—The Mind-Body Connection,* Warner Books, USA.
Eckhart Tolle 2005, *A New Earth,* Penguin Group, Camberwell, Victoria, Australia.
Brian Tracy 1994, *The Psychology of Achievement,* (audio), Sound Ideas, New York.
Dr Denis Waitley 1995, *The Psychology of Winning,* (audio), Sound Ideas, New York.

CLAUDE MIRAGLIOTTA
SEPTEMBER 2007

Introduction

As a child I grew up around the lobster fishing industry of Western Australia. This was in the late fifties and early sixties when fishing boats still weren't fast, but they were considered graceful. By the time I was a teenager they'd started to become more high-tech, with just an inkling of the boats we see today.

Our family's philosophy was one of hard work and frugalness. It was only later I realised that there was never any talk about dreams of success.

Initially I didn't notice any sort of lack. At the time I was totally enthralled by lobster boats, the ocean and the Port of Fremantle, as well as the Swan River. The Fishing Boat Harbour and the river were places of pure adventure for a young boy. It was only when I was about nine that some of this romanticism faded a little. I started to notice that other kids talked about things that we never mentioned at our home—holidays and toys that I could only ever dream of.

Our family environment was not my parents' fault. Their outlook and experience of life was derived from surviving the Great Depression and World War II. Of course this outlook was generational. It was handed down to them by their parents, who, in turn, had learnt it from their parents.

Beneath the surface and unbeknown to me I also viewed life from a similar position, even though I thought otherwise. My outlook was affected by scarcity-anxiety. This anxiety perpetuates a lack of trust in life. It creates a core fear that you will not be provided for. Even when things are going well you'll be thinking about the downside that you are certain will come.

This fear was common during the Great Depression. It was brought to consciousness because of the brutal reality of the time. Like many of the people from that era my parents and grandparents were never taught to consider opportunities. To have a dream and fulfil it was a notion alien to them.

Today, or in any generation, it's no different; this fear—this quiet desperation—still lurks beneath the surface of the minds of many. Even though I thought that I was different, that I could recognise opportunity and take advantage of it, it was only after a marriage break-up that I realised my outlook on life was similar to that of my parents and grandparents.

Scarcity-anxiety usually works in direct partnership with low self-esteem, which in turn can't help but present to us a poor view of our self and of life. Long term, it can result in unsuccessful relationships, poor education and unfulfilling employment. It also has a direct effect on our mental and physical health.

In my case scarcity-anxiety and low self-esteem saw me go through two unsuccessful marriages and the loss of my assets. It created years of ill-health including chronic lower back pain, as well as anxiety and depression. Semi-illiteracy was also part of my daily struggle.

My second marriage came to an end some sixteen weeks after failed back surgery. I found myself alone. From this point on I was mostly bedridden for two years. The majority of my meals had to be eaten lying down or standing up because of the terrible pain I experienced when sitting.

This book is not an autobiography. It explains some of my life situations and some of my struggle. It is essentially a book about the art of overcoming. I've written it for those who seek a better life.

Today I'm not the person I used to be—I'm far better. I'm not a lobster fisherman anymore, nor am I illiterate. I'm a writer and an experienced investor in the stock market. I also supervise exams for financial planners and stockbrokers. I'm in a wonderful loving relationship with my darling Zita. It's the way I always thought a relationship should be: loving, supportive, humorous and exciting. We recently celebrated our fifth year together and we're looking forward to many more.

As I said, it's a book about overcoming.

1

The Beginning

IT WAS THE day my life changed. I'll never forget it. It was altered in a fundamentally wonderful and adventurous way.

We were well into the middle of spring on the fifth day of October 1995 and I was lying in bed as I had done for almost a year. It had been 18 months since I'd last been able to work and earn a living. The reason: debilitating lower back and sciatic pain.

I first experienced the pain when I was 36, and here I was now, nine years later, bedridden. My wife and I were struggling to survive on a disability pension as we watched our savings disappear. We had $2000 in the bank and $1500 worth of bills, with others due to arrive any day. The more I thought about our situation the more fearful I became.

How does one end up in this sort of situation in their middle age? The reason I was in bed was certainly because of back pain. Conventional medicine would say if you work hard physically for over 20 years there is a reasonable chance of incurring a back injury. I discovered only later that work wasn't necessarily the cause of my pain—the cause went much deeper.

Over the previous nine years I had spent a lot of money trying to cure my back problems, but no matter where I went or what I tried, they just got worse. Added to this was long-standing neck pain, which first showed up when I was 18 years old. It had deteriorated to the point where I couldn't turn my neck to the left. When I did so, I experienced sharp stabbing pains in the base of my skull. The pain also ran down the inside of my left shoulder blade and affected my thoracic area. All I could see was a bleak future with very little hope.

My pessimistic outlook, though, had really begun to form 14 years earlier, immediately after my first marriage ended. My wife informed me suddenly one day that, after eight years of marriage, she was leaving. I was devastated. We had three young children between the ages of 13 months and six years. At that time having a wife and family were the most precious things in my life.

I managed to gather myself together to keep functioning. I had a lobster boat, which I owned and operated seven days a week during the season, weather permitting. There were also other people who depended on me for their income, and this was one of the reasons I managed to carry on.

But, as time passed, each day became a struggle to get out of bed, let alone find the energy to work. I didn't see anything to look forward to. Because of this I was sinking into despair. No longer having a marriage was shattering. It understandably left me mourning for what was lost. But I really couldn't comprehend the depth of my depression. Even the light blue waters of the Indian Ocean, which I had loved since I was a small boy, failed to inspire me anymore—all those beautiful, balmy days that used to take my breath away.

I'd seen divorce happen to other people. A few suffered as badly as I did but most went on to create new lives that they were relatively happy with. What was it that made me, and others like me, suffer so much? It was a question I asked myself many times over the following years. Eventually the answers began to reveal themselves.

Not long after the break up another problem emerged—anxiety. This would initially manifest itself as trembling in my stomach.

Within minutes I'd experience a severe drop in energy. The symptoms would then quickly spread through the rest of my body, leaving me with shaky hands, which made it difficult to write.

Over the next six months my mental state deteriorated to the point where I attempted suicide on two occasions. This is the first time I've spoken publicly about it, because it was a source of shame for a long time. I am writing about it to show that this can happen to anyone. But it can only happen when certain things are missing.

We've seen the same thing occur throughout history, to people who have ordinary lives, to those who are highly educated, and to famous people who appear to have it all.

I came to the conclusion that **suicide is the result of life foundations not being built into the core of our character**.

I decided to go about setting up these foundations for myself, to change certain aspects of my personality. Over time the changes I made allowed me to see life from an entirely different perspective. These changes are the key to creating a life that is full of love and true happiness.

If you trust with your heart in the process described in this book, and follow through with persistence (the most important ingredient), you will begin to experience a more optimistic outlook.

Part of my approach to create change included the study and application of metaphysics, as well as practising Buddhist and Transcendental meditations. And even though I was not interested in becoming religious I did draw on some of the core values of Buddhism and Christianity.

Now I remember, as I lay there in bed on that day in October, how beautiful and sunny it was. The flowers were at their peak in the garden and the air was alive with the sound of bush birds, which drifted over from the native park across the road. But for me, none of it meant much. I was unable to raise my spirits because of the continual pain that I was experiencing.

Just as I was despairing about all the springs I would never enjoy, the doorbell rang. It was my sister Nancy. She had come to try to cheer me up; it was going to be a difficult task. As it turned out it was a double surprise because she had brought me a gift. It was a book: *The Power is Within You* by Louise L. Hay. Nancy explained that when she saw it she immediately felt it was for me.

I dragged myself out to the family room to join Nancy and my second wife Ann for a cup of tea. They left the three-seater lounge for me to lie on, because sitting was too painful for me. But sometimes, every once in a while, I would experience periods where the pain would almost disappear. It might just be for half an hour, or several hours. During these times my heart would leap for joy and I would yearn for the old days when I was young and strong.

This sort of thing had been happening for as long as I'd had the injury. I once asked my doctor why this occurred. He explained that sometimes the protruding disc would retract. This would then take the pressure off the sciatic nerve. Depending on how much it retracted would then determine whether the pain stopped or reduced. I was advised to avoid lifting, bending or sitting down. Rest was the main thing that was recommended.

The two surgeons I saw later had similar opinions. My scans showed that I had a protrusion, but not enough to require surgery. I asked if I would be able to work again. The answer was not physically, as I had done in the past. And if I wanted to do any other kind of work, which required sitting or standing, then I would have to get to the point where I could manage those activities.

I tried extensive physiotherapy next. I was treated approximately three times a week for three months as well as having an exercise plan to follow. When certain exercises started to aggravate my back they would be deleted from my program. By the end of the three months there weren't many exercises left that I could do. At this point I decided to stop the therapy because I wasn't experiencing any benefit, in fact, the very opposite was true.

Later, I started a program at another physio centre, which included hydrotherapy and breathing techniques. The experts told me I was not breathing properly or holding myself correctly. In the end that, too, had to be stopped, because most of the exercises increased my pain. I believe that we already know instinctively how to walk, breathe and hold ourselves.

As soon as Nancy left I was keen to begin reading the book. Ann was going out, so I went to the bedroom and settled into my familiar place in bed—which was becoming more and more like my home. It was a home that I was starting to despise with each passing day.

When I started reading I came across terms such as 'God', 'universal power', 'inner wisdom', 'intelligence' and 'infinite mind'. This 'God' word was a problem for me. I'd been brought up as a Catholic, at least until the age of 11. My father was christened a Roman Catholic and my mother was christened in the Church of England, but neither of them practised their religion.

My parents decided that my sister Nancy and I would go to our local Catholic church on Sunday mornings. After about two years I grew to hate this ritual. I never felt it was a place of love, and I couldn't understand why I was always being made to feel sinful.

I don't have a particular problem with the church or any mainstream religion for that matter. But in hindsight their core messages could have been conveyed with a softer, more loving approach, one that didn't frighten the young, or impose such guilt.

Before I'd read very much of the book I was already telling myself that this was going to be airy-fairy. After all, what could it possibly have to do with day-to-day living? Try praying for financial assistance when you have a mortgage with interest rates that are crippling you. And what if you have a serious or terminal illness? No 'power' was going to help anyone with that. I'd seen enough evidence of suffering in the world—I'd been in the middle of my own suffering for at least nine years. We had lost our beautiful house on a one-acre property two years earlier due to my illness, and now we weren't far from losing the smaller home we currently lived in.

I considered material of this kind to be either religious zeal, cult-based, dangerous, or an outright con. But there was something that convinced me to continue reading. I felt that within the pages there were answers to my questions. I also felt a little better after reading a paragraph that gave me the choice of substituting the word 'God' for one that I felt more comfortable with. This approach appealed to me. I chose 'intelligence'; I could live with that.

As with anything in life there are those who will take advantage of others and they are to be avoided. At a specialist bookstore, ask for the most highly-regarded authors in the area of personal growth and spiritual development. When you begin to read their work you will find it has a certain ring of truth about it. I believe we inherently know when we are being lied to or told the truth. Above all, keep your feet on the ground. A healthy, sceptical mind is necessary but not one so sceptical that it blinds you to the truth.

When one's mind is overly suspicious it's operating out of fear, and fear can blind us to opportunity. In this book, as in other material in this field, there will be advice that appeals to you and seems just right—use it. At other times suggestions may seem completely wrong for you—ignore those suggestions. Healing is an individual process.

We are all at different points in our life's journey. Advice that doesn't suit you today may do so in the future. This is not a competition with anyone else. There is no rush. Remember that this is a lifetime's work. The important thing is that you make a start.

As I read more of the book I discovered that, rather than wanting to put it down, I felt compelled to turn the page. Questions would form in my mind and then, as if someone were listening to me, the answers would appear in the next page or two. This is the one thing I have found with all reading in this area. When we are on the path of growth the answers continue to present themselves. The directions forward are not always clear, but if we are willing we will eventually be guided to where we must go.

I reached a section in the book on affirmations. Affirmations are positive statements we tell ourselves about outcomes we want to happen. The one thing that was clear from my reading was the importance of always stating them in the present tense, first person (I am, I have), as if what you want already exists.

At that moment I understood clearly the full meaning of what I had read, and all my scepticism and doubt seemed to vanish. I don't know why this happened but that's the way I felt. I put the book down and began creating an affirmation for my back. Today I can't recall the exact words I used but it was along the lines of, 'I have a very strong, healthy and flexible lower back and spine'.

Once I had that set in my mind I checked to make sure I was still alone and then I closed the windows so the neighbours wouldn't think I was crazy. Apparently it was more effective if you stated an affirmation out loud, especially with strong feeling. And so I began. 'I have a very strong, healthy and flexible lower back and spine.' Nothing! But for some reason I felt positive, so I continued. On the second attempt something incredible occurred. I experienced an electrical charge that ran along the exact pathway where I normally felt sciatic pain. Quickly I repeated the words, in case I had imagined the sensation. There it was again. It felt electrical, yet very pleasant at the same time.

After repeating the affirmation twice more I experienced the very same reaction. This frightened me initially. I didn't know what to make of it. I lay there for at least 20 minutes before repeating it a further five times. The reaction was the same, only the electrical charge was more muted. So, with the different intensities and a 20-minute rest in between, I satisfied myself that what I was feeling was real.

When my wife came home I excitedly told her what had happened and she was genuinely happy for me. I continued reading with great interest thinking that with the reaction I had experienced I would find a cure by the end of the book. Unfortunately I was to discover that the transformation of healing wasn't going to happen that quickly. In some instances it does but this was not to be in my case. I now think that healing in general occurs in steps as we move forward and grow emotionally and spiritually. Even though no cure had arrived by the time I read the last page I was still excited at the prospect of overcoming my situation.

Over the next 12 months I read a further ten books on metaphysics. In addition to reading I found another medium that was very effective: audiotapes. The wonderful thing about audio is that it can be replayed many times so that the message is driven deep into the subconscious. You might try turning off your car radio when you have at least 15 minutes of driving time ahead of you. This is a great opportunity to turn your car into a classroom. Recently, CDs have become more widely available; they produce better sound quality and are more reliable in the long term.

With these tools there is no excuse for those who say they don't have time. Another opportunity to learn is when you are preparing a meal or washing the dishes. Listening to inspirational speakers becomes a meditative experience. I also found that playing certain types of music while I repeated affirmations was relaxing. It seems to allow the mind to absorb the meaning of the words.

It was hard to maintain faith in affirmations—were they really capable of achieving anything? It was only my experience with the back affirmation that kept me going. Because of this there was always a faint belief that what I was doing was right and that I would eventually succeed. The problem was when the pain increased, my belief diminished. At these times doubt would flood my mind. Was I kidding myself? How could I possibly go against expert medical opinion?

When my first marriage broke up I experienced several anxiety attacks each day. Sometimes an attack would continue for 24 hours. Initially I was treated with an antidepressant. The prevailing theory was that I had a chemical imbalance, so with the application of the right medication the balance would be restored. Over time it was hoped that I could get back to normal functioning. Once balance was restored the plan would be to continue on a moderate to low dose and, hopefully, no medication at all eventually.

The theory had sounded fine to me and I was hopeful that it would calm my nervous system. After three months the drug had me feeling worse and even less in control of myself. At the six-month point I stopped taking it. It was also difficult being on this medication whilst skippering a lobster boat, because it left me with dulled senses. I believed this was dangerous for me, my crew and other boat users.

A few years later, even though I was studying metaphysics, which indicated good health could be achieved through natural means, I still thought it unwise to ignore what mainstream medicine had to offer. At this point I decided I needed some help so I paid a visit to my new doctor. When I explained my former and current situation she suggested one of the new antidepressants. After six weeks of medication there was no apparent improvement so I was switched to another drug. Once again the result over a similar period was much the same.

At the end of this period I was referred to a psychiatrist because, as my doctor explained, it was beyond her training to resolve the situation. I was reluctant at first but then I reasoned that I might just strike the right person to help me.

The psychiatrist I saw was a pleasant, approachable man. However, I was disappointed after our initial one-hour interview when he told me I was suffering a chemical imbalance. His approach was one of medication and therapy. After some consideration I agreed to treatment. My thinking was that maybe I gave neither the original, nor the recent, medication long enough to take effect, and therapy might resolve some issues that were driving my symptoms. This time, I decided, I would give treatment every opportunity to work.

I had been told that with my genetic make-up I was predisposed to this type of illness. My father had always suffered with his nerves; he was known to be an emotionally volatile man. There were other family members who were affected by nervous conditions. And so, with a family history and medical opinion, my belief was complete—it was genetic. The advice I was given was that there were things I could do but that I would always need medication because I was predisposed to anxiety problems.

Looking back, it was fortunate for me that I had started looking into metaphysics. Metaphysics is about ultimate intelligence or God—life itself and our connection with it. This connection is limited in the physical sense. It is achieved more on a spiritual level; in fact, it is the dominant way we create our physical reality. We do this by using our mind and working through our heart. You cannot experience regular happiness and joy until you learn to give to yourself and to others.

When you have love in your heart then wonderful things begin to flow into your life. There is no half way. You can't be loving towards some people and hateful towards others, it simply doesn't work that way.

After two years of studying metaphysics and meditating I started to view problems and misfortune differently. It became apparent to me that it really was an opportunity to learn, and to grow. Although this wasn't always clear, I at least stopped thinking that life was conspiring against me. A faint feeling developed in me that life was actually on my side. I also found that it was most often after the event that I would see the lesson.

As you are experiencing a problem situation, know that it will pass and you will learn from it. On some occasions you may not see the lesson, but taking this learning attitude removes a lot of fear, anger and resentment from negative experiences.

We tend to go through pain when we avoid growth. This pain is a result of our resistance to the natural flow of life. Some of the main areas of resistance can occur at the spiritual, emotional, physical, financial and relational levels. The more we attempt to control the things around us, the more pain tends to show up in our lives. It is only when we give up the fight for control that we start to enjoy the full beauty and joy life has to offer.

Giving up the fight doesn't mean that we become passive and dull. In fact, the opposite is true. Our energy levels begin to rise, life develops more flavour and our enthusiasm for it grows. We start to recognise opportunity where once we saw only fear and a lack of hope.

Over the next 12 months I was given a range of high-powered medications, including cocktails of up to three antidepressants at a time. At one point the psychiatrist said he was giving me enough medication to slow down three people and yet it was having little or no effect on my anxiety. I was, however, experiencing slower reaction times when driving my car, and I found this worrying.

During visits I was also receiving psychoanalysis. This consisted of me reading aloud what I had written in a journal between visits. The idea was to cover thoughts about situations that arose during the normal course of events and to express how I felt about them.

By the time 12 months had passed I found that my anxiety had not reduced. In some ways I was more anxious. About one or two hours before a dose of medication was due I would become increasingly nervous and feel as though I might lose control if I didn't take some soon. I understood enough to know that this was partly addiction and I wanted no part of it. It was clear to me that one or all of the medications were perpetuating the anxiety.

When I saw that there was no improvement after this length of time I told the doctor that I no longer wanted to take the medication. I had already begun Buddhist meditations a few months earlier. I knew that many full-time meditators displayed an air of calm and often seemed at peace with life. This knowledge sharpened my desire to find a way to heal. I, too, wanted to experience some peace of mind.

There had to be a better approach, one that didn't leave me feeling drugged and out of control, the way I felt on medication.

The psychiatrist didn't approve of me coming off the medication but in the end he agreed to it. He recommended that I gradually wean off the drugs over six weeks to avoid any reaction. When this was done, I felt a great sense of relief just knowing that I wasn't on antidepressants any more. After two more visits the doctor said that there was little else he could do for me, but that if I had a problem, I could always come back.

As I walked out of his office I felt fearful about what I was going to do next, but at the same time there was a wonderful sense of relief, almost as if I had been let out of jail. I took heart from something the Dalai Lama once said in an interview about depression and such disorders. He commented that these illnesses were not experienced in his society. Yet modern medicine tells us that depression affects all races of people. When asked how they would treat someone from Tibet who was suffering depression he laughed and suggested meditation would be advised. But he was still quite adamant that it was something that just didn't occur in Tibet.

With the knowledge that depression and anxiety, and related illnesses, were prevalent in developed western societies, one had to ask why they were not a problem in Tibetan society. My thoughts immediately turned to the environment. Mentally I quickly hung on tight to that piece of information.

Wisdom tells us that pain is increased when we see and think of ourselves purely as individuals. This is often the case in the developed world because as individuals and as societies we have neglected our spiritual connection to one another. I'm referring to the part in us that is deep within. It is also the part that is connected to life on every level. We are like individual raindrops that fall upon the earth and become part of streams, rivers, lakes and oceans—we are connected to all of life. When we tackle the world alone it is a battle, yet if we reach out with love to life we begin to feel supported. It's then that fear starts to reduce and adventure takes its place.

Even though I was afraid, there was something somewhere inside me telling me that I was safe. Giving me strength were the books of inspiration and wisdom that I had read. The stories of those who had overcome the odds encouraged me. I saw no physical evidence of healing, and yet I felt something was happening beneath the surface, so I continued. The words, 'This is a lifetime's work', made me reassess my timeframe for healing.

2

Change

FOR MANY PEOPLE, starting something new comes with the expectation of getting results straight away. If those results aren't forthcoming they tend to lose heart. Some might try several more times and still not succeed. At this point they either give up, or continue making the same mistakes. The end result is recurring failure.

All that is needed is more information and strategies for correcting those mistakes. When we learn from mistakes and reapply ourselves, the chances of success increase dramatically. In fact, if we persist after each apparent failure, it really is impossible to fail. It's only when we don't get up after each setback that we are truly defeated.

For those who choose to pick themselves up after each disappointment, adjust their plans, and head towards their goal, the reward is the realisation of their dreams. If you think about it, it can't be any other way. Of course, I'm talking about a very determined belief in fulfilling those dreams.

In life, as in healing, things tend to function differently from the way we were taught. But the good thing is, when we discover the rules, we start to gather positive momentum and move forward towards our destiny.

Once you make the decision to expect more out of life, instead of hoping something wonderful will happen one day, then there is only one other important step you will need to take. I know from personal experience and from others who have transformed their lives that change can't be achieved unless **you are the one who changes**. It is only when you come to terms with this fact that you can develop the life you really want.

Making changes within yourself can alter your life in the most profound way. Small consistent changes in your thinking will have an exponentially positive effect on your life and those around you. Remember that you don't have to change anyone else. You don't have to convince others of the rightness of your quest.

After reading my first few books in the personal growth and metaphysical fields, I realised that I had already begun my journey of change some five years earlier. It was in 1990, which was the Australian Year of Literacy. A government commercial was screened on TV, encouraging those who wanted to improve their literacy levels to phone the number advertised.

My partial literacy was something that had bothered me for a long time. You see, I left high school halfway through my first year. I was 14. My competency was already lacking compared to the standard my peers had reached, and this was partly because I was kept down a grade in primary school.

In Year Two of primary school we had a split class made up of Year One and Two students. Unbeknown to my parents, I was mistakenly given Year One lessons again. Missing out on Year Two fundamentals soon showed up the following year. When the records were checked, the mistake was discovered. It was decided to keep me back in the current class, so that I might consolidate.

Painful as this was, it was made even worse by my Year Three teacher. She stood me and another student up in front of the whole class and informed them that we had let everyone down and that we were being kept back. I recall her saying that we'd not tried hard enough, unlike the rest of the children. This stunned me because in my mind I'd applied myself enthusiastically and I thought I was going along okay.

At such a young age a child is very believing. In our formative years, if we are not nourished in a positive way, then it is unlikely that we will develop a core inner strength. From this experience I began to see myself as not good enough; to believe that I was below average.

As I went through the next two years I would find evidence to show that I was right. All around I noticed other children who were smarter than me. They were better at arithmetic. The majority seemed to read more fluently and were further developed with their handwriting. This only served to deepen my feelings of inferiority.

But there was one thing I discovered I was good at, and that was sport. Finally, here was a thread I could cling to—something I could do well. I excelled at athletics and football and almost every other sport I tried. Whatever I did came so naturally. But, looking back, there was a downside to my success. It tended to reinforce my belief that I must be mentally slow and therefore suited only to physical tasks.

In Years Five and Six I improved scholastically but I felt I always had to work much harder than other students to achieve the same results. My grades had slowly advanced to the point where they qualified me to be in 'A' class (the top class) for the final year of primary school. According to my mother, however, I created a fuss and refused to join the class. At a meeting with the headmaster I stated my strong dislike for the teacher as my reason for not wanting to do so. The headmaster was an understanding man and reluctantly allowed me to go to the 'B' class. I was so relieved. The truth was that I thought I was not good enough to be with the top students.

My self-image whispered, 'You can't possibly go in there, you're not as smart as they are. They're going to make you look stupid all over again'. It only became clear to me in my fifties that I had completely accepted the picture I created of myself back in Year Three—whether it was true or not.

In the final year of primary school I finished top of my class. Yet as I packed my bag on that last day, knowing that I would soon be heading to high school, I believed I was not good enough to be going there. I was sure the teachers had made another mistake, and it wasn't really me who was the top student.

During my time at school I had always seen so clearly the things that I could not do. At no time had I ever considered praising myself for what I could do well academically. I was good at history, geography, social studies and writing stories. The trouble is I never allowed those positive self-images to play on my internal screen.

To blame all this on the error of one teacher and the insensitivity of another would be unfair, although that's exactly what I did for a large part of my life. My feelings of inferiority were like buoys anchored beneath the ocean. It only took one of life's storms for them to break loose and float to the surface. Some might place the entire responsibility in the lap of my parents, but that would also be unjust. They certainly always did the best they could for me with the knowledge they had at the time.

Obviously the seeds of inner strength are sown in the environment one grows up in. But how would a parent know anything about developing a child's self-esteem, if they hadn't been taught the skills themselves? As well as our teachers and our home environment, we also have the rest of the world to deal with as our personality develops. The truth is there are few of us who grow up in the ideal situation to build lasting self-esteem.

It's only when we become aware and choose to increase our knowledge beyond our present understanding that we can acquire a different perspective on life. **In the end this is our responsibility,**

not someone else's. This choice will most likely take place sometime during adulthood, if of course we are looking for a better life. Taking personal responsibility will result in a very interesting and satisfying experience of the world. If we do this as individuals we will become more loving, better functioning adults. We'll then create the possibility of having a positive impact on the world.

Sounds fanciful, you say? Not at all. A positive step in our own lives can have an enormous effect on us and the lives of others.

Remember, we must take responsibility to begin the process of change. We can't spend the rest of our lives blaming others. If we do, we'll be forever trapped where we are right now.

After telephoning the number advertised on TV, I was soon transferred to a local college. Even though I was still working at the time, I wasn't able to sit in class with any comfort because of my back. The college was quite happy to start me off with a correspondence course on general literacy.

I found the work interesting and I absorbed the knowledge like a thirsty sponge. Some of the study was done sitting at my desk, but much of it was completed lying in bed. Three years later, back pain forced me to stop working, but I still continued to complete correspondence courses.

By the time I had read Louise Hay's book I'd finished my ninth course. After submitting one particular English assignment, my tutor wrote back and said she was jumping up and down with excitement. She told me that I had the ability to write, and that she had shown a piece of my work to the tutors in creative writing. They agreed with her, and I was advised to join writing classes as soon as possible. Later, I went on to complete a number of writing courses, including an advanced short story program. Having a couple of my short stories published was proof to me that change was taking place.

Since my experience with the first back affirmation, things seemed to be moving forward. My excitement was high and I expected great results. Twelve months later, however, very little appeared to be happening; in fact, my back began to get worse. I was losing heart, and everything in my life seemed to be sliding backwards.

When it appears that you are stagnating it is useful to review your life situation. I do this every six months or so. It helps to give a sense of perspective and direction. If you decide to change your life you will first have to set out your core values and goals. I will discuss this later in the book. It's the reassessing of this structure that will give you a sense of whether or not you are moving forward. Identifying things you have healed and achieved will give you the courage to persist, and to continue moving towards your dream. Even if the progress seems slow or non-existent at first, if you have been applying yourself, analysis will uncover improvements.

By themselves, some of these advancements may seem small, but when you identify a number of them you will realise that real progress is being made. As you detect change in more than one area you will sense that you are beginning to pick up momentum. Often people don't notice this improvement until they bring awareness (analysis) to the situation.

Looking back over periods of six to 12 months generally reveals whether change has occurred. If we work with shorter time spans we find the picture is not so clear. Life is full of cycles and we need to give ourselves time to gain a clearer view of where we are within each cycle. **If we have put positive actions in place, based on an honourable goal, then our progress can only be judged over the longer term.** With shorter time spans we tend to be caught up in current emotions. Because of this, we can't make clear judgements.

An analogy would be a quality share in the stock market that has fallen in price. If we own the stock at the time of its plunge we are immediately affected by the emotion of the moment. The emotion is fear. We fear that we may lose our money. If we were considering buying the share for the first time, we begin to fear that if we buy it, and it falls, we will have paid too much. On the other hand we may be afraid that if we don't buy quickly enough it could go up and we will miss out. So as you can see our short-term view can be clouded by emotion.

What to do? With our lives, as it is with a stock, the only way we get to the truth is by analysis. One of the first things we do with a share is look at the research. We check to see if the management team is still in place and working well together. Is the business model sound and on track, and viable in the current climate? How is the outlook for earnings?

An experienced investor in the market is not upset by short-term fluctuations. They take the long-term view. They are supported in their outlook when they have a plan in place. Don't ever be deterred by short-term events in your life. Know that your healing is progressing if your plan is in place.

It is important that we do our research when reviewing our life. Firstly, look at the areas that you have intended to improve in. For example, it may be correcting a bad habit of criticising yourself. Have you improved in that area? One way of knowing is to ask yourself: am I more supportive of myself now? If the answer is yes, then you can be sure that your true self is beginning to emerge from beneath the other layers of your personality. Over time you will develop more compassion and affection.

The Dalai Lama advises in *The Little Book Of Wisdom*, that if we allow our natural qualities of compassion and affection to expand in our mind, we are in effect practising 'spirituality'.

Remember, as you develop love in your heart for your self, you will most certainly have it to give away to others. These qualities are inborn, but don't expect to consistently exhibit them overnight. The process of healing takes time. Have patience. As you become more conscious of your self-criticism you will at the same time start to practise compassion and human affection. These feelings lead to further improvement in one's life.

As we begin to concentrate on what we want in our lives, and not what we *don't* want, those things start to come towards us. In this case, we stop focusing on self-criticism. Instead we make it our practice to focus our minds on being self-supportive and compassionate.

A similar approach can work with others. You might like to try this within a relationship you are seeking to improve. Look for some good points in the person's character, and let these permeate your mind, rather than the things you don't like about them. Then begin to compliment them on those very things, even if it feels unnatural at first. What you are doing is ignoring your own prejudice. You are looking to connect with that person's true inner core, which is love.

Take the time to do something nice for this person without expecting them to express gratitude. This may be hard at first—but do it anyway. As you give a compliment, mean it in your heart. While you are going about this, be aware of your thoughts. If your thoughts are not in alignment with what you say and do, then correct those thoughts.

In essence, we are talking about *intention*. Check your intention in every situation. It is an accurate gauge to see if you are offering love or hate. By taking this approach you may experience a positive change in attitude from others (not necessarily from everyone, because we are all at different points on our spiritual journey). This is the natural development of respect. Respect is a crucial component of love.

I would ask you to be persistent and have faith in this exercise. You must remove your ego from the process. The ego will be looking for a pat on the back for being such a Good Samaritan. If it doesn't come, it will immediately blame the other. Once again, this attitude will leave you stuck right where you currently are. If there is to be change in your life, you are the one who must begin that change—not the other. You may find the other person will eventually go out of your life, but it will be with a sense of gratitude in each of your hearts. Bitterness will no longer be part of who you are.

You can also develop a positive intention towards your own health by creating a visualisation. Create a picture in your mind of a fit, trim and healthy you—**develop it so it is crystal clear**, this is most important. You might like to sit somewhere peaceful for five or ten minutes, once or twice a day. With your eyes closed, visualise this wonderful image.

Remember, this suggestion is only part of the answer to developing the healthy body you desire. Coming to know your self on the spiritual level will lead to a deep love and gratitude for the body you have been given. This will then blossom into respect and understanding for just how divine this gift really is. Once you develop respect for something, you will not harm it.

When I was bedridden, I created a picture of myself enjoying vibrant early morning walks by the river. In another, I saw myself riding a beautiful black mountain bike, up and down hilly roads, just like an excited kid. This was even though I hadn't been able to ride a bike for almost 13 years. Each time I attempted to ride I ended up with incredible lower back and sciatic pain. As a result, I would find myself bedridden for periods of two weeks or more.

I held these positive pictures and many others lovingly in my mind. Through the days of pain and hopelessness, I clung to them like a lifeline. Those days became years. But I maintained and nourished my pictures, and eventually they became my reality. If you practise consistently, pictures will start to develop and they will become clearer. Those pictures will eventually become your beliefs. In time they will manifest physically, often in the most mysterious ways. Just thinking about a subject is a form of visualisation, so don't worry if you don't see pictures in the beginning.

Shakti Gwain in her book *Creative Visualization* proposes that thought is a form of energy. She suggests that concentrating on a thought or idea will begin the process of attracting its equivalent into the physical realm. So the thoughts, ideas and pictures in your mind are in fact visualisations. The only difference with a formal visualisation is that you have a specific time to focus on a particular goal.

For a few years I complained to myself that I couldn't master the technique of visualisation. My advice to you is—practise it anyway. Learning to focus our mind in this way also teaches us about awareness. Most of us are not fully aware during our waking hours. We think we are conscious but often our mind is somewhere else. Have you ever been driving in your car and gone a couple of streets past where you wanted to turn off? You know the route intimately; you've been there countless times. That's your mind on holiday from the present—it's not in the here and now. If you were conscious, fully in the moment, you would have turned at the correct street.

Learn to become aware of where your mind really is—whether it's driving to a destination or any task you may be involved in. Is your mind present? Because if it's not you won't be applying yourself to the best of your ability, you won't be giving it everything you've got.

I think Shakti Gawain is correct when she describes an idea as a blueprint. Ultimate intelligence then mobilises energy to manifest the physical form of that blueprint. This is how my mountain-bike visualisation became reality for me—through my persistent visualisation I mobilised the energy for my body to heal (manifested form), which allowed me to ride free of pain.

Some thoughts are unconscious. Remember that this can still be occurring in picture form. These pictures happen so quickly that most people don't realise they are there. It's only when the mind focuses on one thought for a while that we become conscious of the picture. Negative thoughts can therefore be part of a visualisation that creates a depressive life. When you doubt your ability, that doubt reinforces these negative pictures in your mind.

Very early in my metaphysics studies, Dr Denis Waitley confirmed this for me in his audio series *The Psychology of Winning.* He explained what happened when actors were connected to electrodes and blood catheters. When they played a sad part, their vital signs were adversely affected and endorphin production dropped. The opposite was true when they played a happy, joyful part. Not only were their vital signs steady, along with an increase in endorphin production, but they actually felt happy.

Endorphins are biochemical compounds that produce a natural analgesia and a sense of wellbeing. Dr Waitley's evidence clearly demonstrates how our thoughts can affect our health and therefore our life.

The fact is that when you think of an apple, you don't picture the word 'apple'. You actually see an apple in your imagination. When you were a child and you were afraid of the monster under your bed, what did you see? I'll bet it wasn't the word 'monster' printed in large letters in your imagination. It would've been an image of a monster, in a place that was dark and frightening. This darkness would have evoked all sorts of possibilities in your imagination.

You might understand now that you've been visualising your whole life. What thoughts do you have in your mind about your body, your finances, your relationships or anything else? Whatever dominant thoughts you hold in your mind, you will tend to manifest that physical equivalent in your life.

Ask anyone who has overcome incredible odds in the areas of health or poverty, or recovered from any difficult situation. They will tell you they had a goal—a picture in their minds of how it was going to be for them, and they continued to focus on that picture no matter what their current circumstance was.

Opportunities, and what we want from life, come through our minds. Understanding this idea is most important if we are to create the life we want. We have the gift of free will. We can actually select the life we want by concentrating on the pictures we desire, and then taking physical action towards achieving those images. Many of us have not been taught how to use this beautiful gift effectively. In fact, most of us concentrate on our fears.

The healing path of an individual is much like the chart direction of a quality share. When we look at its price graph over a short period we may find it has fallen in value. This can be worrying. But if we know the rules we also know that in time it will increase in value. Taking the long-term outlook with our life is no different.

The important part of reviewing our plan is being able to make adjustments where they're necessary. As long as your goal is worthy and does not harm or take advantage of others then you will succeed by finetuning your plan along the way. I can tell you it took me a long time to get myself on track with a plan that would work. This was because I was always caught up in short-term thinking (fear). As such I had no real plan in place.

Be encouraging and gentle with your self—this is vitally important. There are enough critics in the world and you've probably been one of your own most severe critics up until now. As you begin to recognise change, you will grow in enthusiasm. Even if a situation appears hopeless, you won't view it that way. Remember, some of the most successful people throughout history came from backgrounds of poverty, illiteracy and adversity. Recognise areas where little or no advancement has occurred and create plans to remedy those situations. As you encounter problems you will begin to look for solutions, rather than thinking that nothing can be done, or that the situation will get worse.

Continue reading and listening to inspirational thinkers. This will entrench the positive suggestions you have already planted in your subconscious. It will teach you to stretch and grow further and will give you greater resolve when you fall. I found that when I was feeling down and affirmations weren't working, or if I didn't have time to read something uplifting, I would listen to inspiring tapes.

This might be any time of the day or night. It could be in the middle of preparing a meal, or driving somewhere. At other times it might be late evening when the stress of the day had built up. It's a great way to relieve accumulated tension.

Avoid people who criticise you or who have a negative outlook on life. If this is not possible, then at the very least close your mind to their pessimistic outlook. You might like to counter this with your own positive thoughts but keep them to yourself. If you convey your new-found optimism to these people it can result in criticism, which in the early stages may well undermine your confidence.

My next suggestion is to be compassionate and empathetic to these negative personalities. As with my earlier suggestion, look for positive points in their character. When you praise these people you will find they start to become less vocal. This is because when a person receives empathy they feel cared for.

My reason for suggesting this is that people who speak in a negative or even aggressive manner are only doing so out of fear. By treating others this way you'll be surprised how some relationships can be transformed into loving, supportive ones.

Once again, those who do not support you in your quest will eventually go out of your life—wish them well. It will take compassion and at times courage to apply this on a regular basis. I'm not saying that we can achieve this all of the time; but holding on to bitterness simply means that, in the end, you are the one who will be harmed by it.

From my studies I knew that belief was an integral part of the healing process. If I held deeply the view that I had a weak and painful back, then that's what would most likely manifest itself. The intention of the positive affirmation in this area was to alter my belief to one of having a strong, healthy and flexible back. My purpose was to actually change my physical reality.

At first I would affirm and then try to do some physical work, but I'd usually end up in bed with agonising back pain. This was because the source of my back pain was coming from an entrenched subconscious belief. No matter how much I affirmed in a positive manner with my conscious mind, I was being defeated by this deep-seated belief.

Established in the far reaches of my psyche was the view that life would never truly provide for me. This was something that I wasn't fully aware of at the time. But now I see I had always had an inkling of this, a feeling that things wouldn't work out financially. The affirmations were having some benefit, but their effect was limited because of my scarcity-anxiety. With this conflict going on they could not take root in my subconscious mind. It is in the subconscious mind where the past incorrect perceptions of life need to be rewritten.

No-one can measure how long this change will take for the individual, because it depends entirely on how deep one's negative views go. Bear in mind that it took you until now to develop your personality to its current stage. Once you become aware and apply yourself, transformation will occur more quickly than you might think.

The only resistance to this change will be in your own mind. We conquer resistance by increasing our enthusiasm for life. Affirmations and visualisations are useful for building initial enthusiasm. Reading about those who have overcome adversity and who inspire us about life reminds us that we are not alone. Through meditation we have a consistent way of reconnecting with our spiritual core. I talk more about meditation in Chapters 3, 5 and 14.

Relationships are also another way of gauging change, especially if you practise the exercise on complimenting and building respect. When you see improvements it will encourage you to continue. But in the end, even the best plan won't work if you aren't willing—so it's up to you. It really does take as much energy to create a life of pain as it does to create a joyful one.

I thought deeply about my lack of trust in life to provide for me. It seemed that on an emotional level it had been true for me as far back as I could remember. I was afraid of being poor and homeless. It was a fear that never really left me. I think there are many of us that carry this fear to varying degrees, and it is not linked to our income or assets. It can be just as true for a wealthy person as it can be for someone who is just getting by.

Scarcity-anxiety is simply to what degree we believe that life will or will not provide for us. Those who expect opportunities to come their way usually experience exactly that, and those who are afraid of what might go wrong rarely see opportunity—even when it's right in front of them.

In my case this belief was passed down through the generations, which is true for most of our beliefs, but not all of them. My parents came from working-class families and grew up in the Great Depression. Dad was born in Australia to Italian parents and Mum was of English stock, born in England. She arrived in Australia by ship at just six months of age.

Growing up, my general impression of money was that it was hard to get and had to be held on to tightly. There always seemed to be the worry of some financial difficulty ahead, and yet that worry was never clearly defined. When I think about my childhood, I don't recall much talk about prosperity or possible opportunities. Our minds were trained, inadvertently, to fear what might go wrong, rather than to see opportunity.

When I began lobster fishing I was determined to gain my financial security. But it was to be a long time before I understood what that word 'security' really meant. After working on the deck for 15 years, I finally took over skippering the boat from my father at the age of 29. I was determined to be more financially successful than he had been, simply because I wanted a better life. I didn't want to have to struggle the way he and Mum had. My outlook was more expansive and so I quickly built a bigger boat and acquired a larger licence.

I was driven to be successful. 'Driven' is a good word to describe the way I lived my life. If one has balance in their life, they are not driven; it is more a matter of inspiration and passion. When a person is inspired, they treat themselves and others with respect.

Looking back now it is easy to understand why I pushed myself so hard; it was scarcity-anxiety. This is the same fear that drives some multimillionaires to earn more and more, even though they are already extremely wealthy. When one is so driven, it usually corresponds with little understanding of the welfare of others. Often, the very driven are not particularly happy with their overall lives. In these cases you generally find that their immediate family life is also stressful.

People who suffer this way are time-poor, and are not able to offer love in their most important relationships—including to themselves. They understand that quality time needs to be put into these relationships, but somehow they never quite get around to it. Fear is driving them so hard because in their mind they're afraid they may lose it all; thus the desire to earn even more. The rationale is that they need to do this to survive any possible disaster that may come along. In time, their life becomes more unbalanced, and they derive even less satisfaction from it.

The thing that causes the fear of scarcity is the belief that we are alone; that life is an individual effort. When we accept this as fact, it then becomes easy to subscribe to the 'pie theory'—get your piece before it's all gone. This theory says if you are not aggressive or quick enough, you won't be able to get your share. When this is the case, it says that life will always be a struggle, with not much to look forward to. Sadly, this is the reality for many people.

Life has little to do with beating others. It's more about what we think of ourselves inside and how we choose to process life. From then on, all that is required of us is to organise our thoughts and actions to bring our chosen beliefs into reality. Those who believe they are not good enough or smart enough will actually experience that reality. I proved this to myself when I looked back at my time in primary school. I was the one who worked hardest at creating failure, even though there was clear evidence to prove otherwise.

Back pain or other conditions or illnesses are no different. These are life's way of telling us that we need to stop what we are doing, and start pursuing our destiny. This may require us to strike out in a different direction. Once we begin, life will guide us, as long as we put our heart and energy into it.

Over time there were increasing problems showing up in my second marriage. It had not been an easy relationship except for the first couple of years. The money situation wasn't helping, but I knew that this was not the cause of our disharmony. I had no idea how to solve the long-term problems that were now coming to a head.

We attended private marriage counselling sessions and also went to group classes, but in the end it made little difference. The same issues came up over and over again. It was as if we were bumping into an invisible wall between us, with no doorway so that we might reach each other.

As our marriage deteriorated, so did my back. From a metaphysical point of view it was just another area where I felt unsupported. During the next year I received further spinal injections, some of which were quite painful. I remember one of them aggravated my back and put me in hospital for two days. I would always be told how this injection would give me pain relief, but at no time did I ever experience any.

During my years of suffering back pain I also tried alternative treatments, such as naturopathy, chiropractic, acupuncture and magnets. There were also other things that now seem pretty silly. One treatment included bouncing on a mini trampoline whilst alternately tapping the right and left nostrils. Another required daily oil baths. I now know from metaphysics and a more commonsense point of view that the more ridiculous one feels about a treatment, the less likely it is to work.

With long-term illness you either give up or search harder for a solution. The level of pain a person is in, and the duration of that pain, often determines a person's desperation for a solution. At this point we are vulnerable to unscrupulous operators in the area of healing. Of course this is when people are least able to make sound judgements about what is being offered. In the end, this is why we need to take responsibility for our lives and to heal the areas that are out of balance. When we do this the body will begin to heal.

During my early years of suffering I found that alcohol calmed the pain I felt deep inside. The problem of course was that this only lasted as long as I was drinking. I knew this was a dangerous course of action and that it could easily lead to alcoholism. I had no intention of going down that road.

There was also a reason why my initially prescribed medication never worked. The problem was I was looking for happiness outside of my self. It was years before I began to understand that I couldn't have peace of mind and happiness unless I first looked inside.

Overcoming pain means facing your fears. At first we do this in small ways. This building of courage is essential, because as our courage grows, so does our resilience to future adversity. People often mistake facing fear with facing pain. Rather than having to be physically tough and overcome pain directly, it is more important to overcome our learned fears. When we do this, physical pain tends to evaporate.

During my years of pain I often asked myself the question: what was this pain that I felt? The answer wasn't forthcoming. I truly had no idea. But what I did know was that other people suffered in their hearts and spirits just as I did. You could see it on their faces or by the way they lived their lives. They might be addicted to drugs, alcohol or smoking. On the other hand they could just as easily be in a difficult relationship, or have financial problems.

Pain will be experienced in any area of life when we avoid growth and seek to stay the same as we are. This is because we're going against the very flow of life.

My intake of alcohol increased quite a bit for 18 months after my first marriage ended. Even so, I was still considered to be a light drinker by the standards of some fishermen. These were tough men, who worked and drank hard and lived their lives fearlessly. More than a few took a casual approach to the health of their bodies.

Having said this, I also admire them, because it takes a certain resilience to work in the conditions they endure. I know—I did it for 21 years. Where we operated from, there was no calm marina. You had to drag your dinghy down the beach each morning from beyond the high water mark. As well as this there were always boxes of bait and gear to carry. You then had to push out through the waves to get to your boat on the moorings. This was often made worse when carried out in darkness.

This book is not about fishermen, alcoholism or substance abuse. Its intention is to show how you can experience a greater level of happiness and joy in your life, when previously all you may have felt was emotional, mental or physical suffering.

If you are a substance abuser, seek medical help for immediate support. I would then encourage you to consider deeply and take to heart the ideas I present in this book. By doing this you will gain a true understanding of how I applied the information I have collected. You will then be able to create change in your life. I know you can do this because there are numerous examples of people throughout history who have achieved exactly that.

Continue searching for other books and materials in the personal growth, metaphysics and spirituality area. You will live an ordinary life but you will begin to live it in a most wonderful way—from your heart. This doesn't mean everyone will love you. It doesn't mean every relationship will go smoothly. But it will ensure that you are living your relationship with life on purpose. A life lived on purpose automatically brings joy, happiness and fulfilment.

One of the problems with our education system is that we are not taught to listen in the right way. We are told to listen with our head and not our heart. But I believe we must first listen with our heart to gain a true feeling for any situation. Once we are in touch with this feeling we need to then apply our intellectual mind to the circumstance. But this intellect must be used in a specific way.

My belief in this approach developed after reading words of wisdom of influential historical figures. Some of these influences were Mahatma Gandhi, Buddha, the Dalai Lama, Jesus, Mother Teresa, Albert Einstein, Alexander Graham Bell, Henry Ford and Thomas Edison. This list also included ordinary people who had overcome the most incredible odds. So, whether they were influential spiritual leaders, great scientists, historic business icons, or the person next door, they all had something in common. They successfully applied the same metaphysical laws to their lives.

Prior to undertaking this reading, I didn't know that there were any metaphysical laws to life. As a child all I understood from my few years at church was that I had to be good and not sin, otherwise something terrible would happen to me. In adulthood, until my early forties, my understanding was that the world was a place where everyone did their best to survive against the odds. I was so glad to discover (although late in life) that our success and happiness is not created in the physical world. It is first created in our minds and then played out in the physical world.

The pain we experience (resistance to the flow of life) means that life is showing us that there is something we must face and overcome before we can move forward. There are no quick fixes to all of our problems and, truly, it is a life's work. But I can tell you it will be the most satisfying and inspirational work you ever do. Sometimes we are aware specifically of what the pain is but mostly we are not, because it is subconscious or semi-subconscious.

Healing and growth can only come from gentle, persistent action with the intention of overcoming our fears. This will correct the wrong perceptions that we have collected over a lifetime. The vast majority of these perceptions are formed in our childhood and early teenage years. Even so, our personalities are still influenced to a certain degree by events in later years.

This last statement is vitally important. It means we have the ability to change, not so much our personalities, but the way in which we interact with the world. We now know that if we are not happy with our life we can choose to have a better life. This choice is truly free will. But it's the correct application of this will, backed by perseverance, which will bring about real and lasting change.

Remember, if you concentrate on financial wealth alone and neglect the other aspects of your life, you will most likely be disappointed. You may be wealthy, but without love and loving relationships you will never find happiness. It's the same as wanting to have a healthy body. You can't fully achieve this just by eating sensibly. Regular exercise must also be part of your plan. It's exercise that gives you vitality and helps increase your enthusiasm. Like all success in life, a multifaceted approach is needed to bring it about.

Most of us would like to be treated with respect, love and gratitude. But this won't happen unless we first apply these things to ourselves, and then to others, each and every day. Life is about balance in all areas—mental, emotional, spiritual, physical and relational. If we only love others and not ourselves we become the victims of lives out of balance.

At this point, with the different stresses in my life, I wasn't making any headway healing my back pain, so I decided to give my mind a rest from trying to heal it for a while. I figured I was concentrating on it so much that I was probably making the situation worse. Even though I understood the scarcity theory and how it related to me, I also knew enough to know that I wasn't likely to change my outlook overnight. So with this in mind I thought I would tackle another illness in my body.

The neck pain which I'd first experienced late in my teens had been with me for approximately 28 years. I thought, why don't I try healing it instead? Even though it was a much longer-standing injury than my back pain, I didn't feel as intimidated by it.

When I looked up neck problems in Louise Hay's book *You Can Heal Your Life*, she suggested attitudes like stubbornness and inflexibility as being the causes of neck pain. After I considered this, I definitely felt that her comments were true for me in both areas.

I understood that altering my outlook in these areas would take some doing, but I was more than willing to work at it. If I accepted the theory that illness in the body was a product of our dominant thoughts, then I should be able to use thought to create a different result with my neck.

Dr Denis Waitley, Louise Hay and others qualified in the field of the mind, suggest that there are thousands of thoughts that pass through our mind every day. Many of these we are unconscious about. I decided to see if I could fill my mind with a particular thought every moment of every hour that I was awake, just for one day. I rationalised that if I could do this, then the thought pattern that continually caused my neck pain would have to retreat, and so, too, would the pain.

The next day I used the affirmation for neck problems in *You Can Heal Your Life*. But rather than the affirmation, it was the causes (stubbornness and inflexibility) that seemed to leave the most impression on me. The book also advocated that there were many ways of doing or seeing any one thing. This started to expand my view on different issues, because I grew up believing there might only be a few ways of doing anything.

I repeated the affirmation silently to myself for most of the day, when I wasn't in the company of others or occupied with some task. The way my life was at the time, there wasn't much company or many tasks to distract me, so I had ample opportunity to work on my theory.

After the first couple of hours I noticed a lessening of my pain, especially when I became enthusiastic about the affirmation—in other words, when I began to believe deeply what I was repeating. At the end of the day I had experienced a considerable reduction in pain. It was enough to fire my imagination. Here I had experienced a real reduction in pain due to applying my mind in a certain way. I immediately tied this in with my first experience of the back affirmation. When I thought about it, I realised what a sustained effort it would take to make an affirmation like that stick, or more importantly, to turn it into a *belief*.

3

Reality

OUR REALITY CAN vary depending on the environment we grew up in. If we were lucky and were raised in a supportive and encouraging atmosphere, then we will probably have a happy, well-balanced life. This type of environment would be the kind in which it was okay to make mistakes, rather than being fearful of them. At the same time, if we were taught that mistakes were an opportunity to learn and to grow, then we will show more creativity than others in our formative and adult years.

When we're creative, we experience a high level of joy, because we are beginning to get on track with our purpose in life. In other words, we're in tune with what life expects of us. Creative adults find themselves engaged in work that fulfils their purpose. This is because their life tends to have a spiritual foundation to it.

Every creative person senses that their most inspired work comes from a place beyond themselves or their teachers. By having this spiritual perspective creative people understand that there is an intelligence that operates within life. It is my belief that this intelligence conducts the workings of the entire universe, including the involuntary functions in our bodies. This intelligence is an eternal living entity and we are a wonderful part of it. Finances are not a problem for creative people because, with their spiritual foundation in place, their life is in balance. When we're in balance we tend to attract the money we need at the time it is needed. It is all to do with life flow. When we're in balance we are going with the energy of life and not against it. Because of this we tend to see opportunities and take advantage of them.

I often used to think in my days of financial struggle that this was a nice theory but it wouldn't pay the bills. The answer to this is that one not only has to gain faith that life is intelligent but also that it's working in our favour. Faith is probably one of the most difficult things to believe in, especially if you have no experience of it.

I began to find faith when I felt a change with the first back affirmation and then when I achieved some reduction in my neck pain. Even though that reduction only lasted for short periods it was enough to make me want to continue. I didn't truly understand at the time that this same faith could be just as easily applied to the area of finance.

It would be difficult for us to believe in ourselves, or in life providing for us, if we grew up in an atmosphere of conditional love. Our parents might say, do this or do that and mummy and daddy will love you. If love was withdrawn, how could a child build self-esteem, or trust in anything? The situation may have been compounded if we were criticised for making mistakes. And it would become foundational if we were continually warned of financial hardship and possible disaster ahead.

Often this is done unintentionally by parents who love their children but lack the skills to create an encouraging environment, one in which they can grow and expand. This is far more likely if those parents were raised in a negative atmosphere themselves.

The environment in which we grow up, whether it is healthy or unhealthy, creates our world view. We then pass this assessment on to our children believing that this is the way the world really is. If we had critical parents and accepted their view of the world, then it's likely we'll be critical of others and ourselves. At the same time, we may also be distrustful of the world. As a result it may mean that we are getting far less satisfaction from life than is available.

The idea that we cannot find peace of mind and happiness externally, in either money or anything else, took me a long time to come to terms with. Happiness can only come from the inner core values of love for our self and for life. Just as importantly, this also includes developing gratitude and respect towards all things in life, ranging from other people, to the food we eat and to the very air we breathe.

While I continued working on my neck and back, it was still difficult for me to admit that it was I who had to change. I eventually got to the point where my back pain became so great I couldn't stand it any longer. In desperation I went to see the top neurosurgeon in Western Australia and he kindly agreed to operate on me through the public hospital system.

Without this assistance I wouldn't have been able to afford him privately. Even though I was grateful for his help, there was still conflict in my mind over trying to heal myself metaphysically, versus the medical option. One has to be careful when taking the metaphysical view. Don't become too stubborn and rule out opportunities from other areas.

I often felt like I was close to conquering my pain. I really wanted to heal naturally. But at the time I couldn't find a way to do so when I needed it most. Unfortunately, surgery turned out to be unsuccessful for me. It left me with higher levels of pain.

Shortly after, the surgeon suggested corrective surgery, because, as he put it, there was a recurrence of the disc protrusion. To my dismay, the hospital wouldn't agree. I believe this was because another high-profile surgeon had just lost a major compensation claim over failed back surgery. In the hospital's view, corrective surgery would have put my case into the higher-risk category. Looking back, the lack of surgical success turned out to be a blessing, because it caused me to look more deeply into the mind–body and spiritual connection.

Four months later, my wife and I separated. The pressure of the failed surgery and the long-term problems in our marriage had become too much. It seemed life was conspiring to teach me some valuable lessons about courage and faith, although I didn't see it that way at the time.

I rented a place close to my family because I knew from past experience that it was important to have a good support base during a difficult time such as this. It was my intention to handle things differently this time around. After my first divorce I was very lonely, partly because I was living 100 kilometres away from my family.

The next three months were difficult, emotionally and physically. I suffered terrible back pain that was often at the limit of what I could manage. I was unable to do much of my housework. Shopping was also painful. During this time I was very thankful for the assistance of my family, especially my two sisters, who occasionally helped with shopping and housework.

I was able to cook for myself but the problem was I couldn't sit down to eat because it caused me such intense pain. The result was that I ate most of my meals lying down. This continued for over two years.

Even though I wouldn't want to go through this period in my life again, it was actually an opportunity. It gave me the chance to reflect and spend time on my own, and to get to know my self better. As I look back it really was a time of great change for me.

The difference the second time around compared to my first divorce was that the emotional pain and despair were not as deep. I realised the reason for this straight away. It was because of the personal growth work I'd already been doing. There was a strength building inside me, and I knew it was directly related to the reading I'd been doing and the affirmations I had worked on.

Another crucial element for me was meditation. Even though I was suffering more physically than at any other time in my life, meditation helped me believe that I would be guided though the pain and eventually overcome the situation. I'm not saying I believed this all of the time, in fact, very often I doubted it. But every time I hit rock bottom this wonderful strength, this belief, would glimmer inside me and I would move forward towards my goals.

Even though I was working at healing I often found myself blaming my first wife for the situation I was in. Looking back on my second marriage, different as it was, the results in some ways were the same. When I say results, I mean how I felt emotionally within those relationships. In both cases there was always a feeling of being unloved. It was a sense of emptiness when I looked deep inside myself. I was waiting for the other to give me love, but it never seemed to come in the way I wanted it to.

As my back continued with what seemed like ever-worsening pain, I began shifting some of that blame on to doctors, surgeons and alternative practitioners. I had not accepted the metaphysical view that illness in the body was a reflection of an imbalance in one's life. Reading wisdom like this and then internalising it takes a considerable shift in thinking, even when one is willing to change. This is because in western societies we are taught to look out there for the solution and not inside, where the true answers are to be found.

In developed countries we have been encouraged to sue the other party if we feel the wrong thing has been done to us. This perpetuates the myth that things are always someone else's fault. It is a course that some people follow their entire life. But if you look closely at some of those courtroom winners over the long term, you will find they often don't gain the satisfaction they hoped for. The pain they experienced continues.

A metaphysical view is: what we perceive in another is part of ourselves reflected back at us. When I was attempting to heal, I found this hard to swallow. What had someone else's bad behaviour got to do with me? I was missing the point! Another person's behaviour is their own problem. It was that word 'reflection' that I had misunderstood. The other person is simply the mirror to help you consider similar behaviour in yourself. It then gives you the opportunity to review your own conduct. Once again it is a chance to grow and improve as a person.

I learnt something about this by accident as I developed a spiritual exercise over a couple of years. It was when I was teaching myself to walk again without pain. It showed me in very simple terms that what we hold in our hearts and in our minds is what we truly get out of life.

During my morning walks I noticed some people would smile and say good morning with enthusiasm on their faces. Their enjoyment and gratitude for their surroundings (life) was very clear. Others would deliberately put their heads down as they approached me. Clearly they wanted no contact.

Over time I began to notice my own emotions as these people approached. From 30 metres away if they were already looking at me and smiling, I noticed my spirits would begin to lift. I found it almost impossible not to respond with a smile and a friendly 'Good morning'. When I saw someone up ahead with a sour look on their face and their eyes cast down at the footpath, there was not the slightest urge in me to say hello.

After a while I decided to be one of the happy people enjoying the fresh morning air. When someone approached me I would hold myself erect and enthusiastically say, 'Good morning!' Initially I had a good response and even a few converts among the unhappy walkers.

Towards the end of the two years I realised part of what I was doing was superficial. It concerned the unhappy walkers. I suddenly became aware that when I first saw them my reaction was, 'What a miserable so and so'. Even though I would present with the enthusiastic greeting, deep in my heart I was not really feeling that way. On the surface I was cheerful, but underneath I was thinking, why should I bother with this person?

When I became aware of this and took action to correct my thinking, things began to change for the better. In the end I decided no matter how they appeared, I would wish them a bright 'Good morning!' because I was happy to be alive and enjoying the beautiful surroundings.

The response was quite amazing. Once I took this course of action towards a walker, I could sense an energy reach out from me and connect with them. In the majority of cases the other person would respond almost magically, even from 30 metres away. This would result in them looking up at me and smiling. At this point I could feel a similar energy to my own coming back from them. In almost all cases they couldn't wait to say 'Good morning'. This now tends to happen automatically and really gives me a great start to my day.

Invisible strings connect us all. We give and receive energy all the time. It's up to us to choose whether we create a positive energy flow or not. It is also our responsibility to limit our exposure to people who constantly criticise and see only the negative things in life.

When you're out walking you might consider this. If you see someone approach you, say to yourself, I'm going to give them the very best greeting I've got. **Mean it in your heart.** Don't be put off by whether they look friendly or unfriendly; just be aware of that positive thought in your heart.

Feel the natural surroundings about you: the warmth of the air, the call of different birds and the colour range of the various plants and trees. Even if it is raining, feel gratitude for it. Remember how you used to like playing in the rain as a child. You only stopped because of learned 'adult' behaviour.

Now! Hold yourself erect and feel great to be alive. Walk with a spring in your step. Irrespective of the response you get, feel happy to be alive. Expect nothing from the other person—this means you must remove your ego from the process.

This exercise may take you some time to achieve positive results; it depends on your attitude at the core level.

When you begin to get the reaction I'm talking about, it will set you up for a much happier day. It will also deepen your appreciation for nature and your connection with others. Over time, the truth that we are all one will begin to grow in your mind. Rather than having resentment for others, you will start to expand in understanding and compassion.

The exercise demonstrates the point that by using our mind we can change a response. One result is that we experience an elated feeling from within ourselves, where previously there wasn't one. The other result comes from outside ourselves when we connect with the other person. This shows the power of the mind to affect our inner and outer world. The changed reaction from the other is most important. It is more than a smile at 30 metres that achieves this. It has everything to do with the energy generated from our intention.

Don't expect a positive response from everyone. You can't change the whole world. But what is certain is that you will increase your own feelings of joy, and this in turn will have a positive effect on a significant number of other people.

Just play with this exercise, as a child might when discovering something new. It's a way of learning about the use and flow of energy. Don't try too hard; it's a fun thing, to gain understanding. You don't have to do this at every opportunity. Sometimes we have a right to feel down. But if you are feeling low and would like a lift, work with this exercise.

How do you treat your self—what is your intention towards *you?* In other words, what is your self-view, if you look beneath the surface of the persona that you present to the world? Are there aspects of the whole that you see as okay and other parts you are ashamed of? Could it be that you are angry about things you see as flaws in your character but have been unable to change? Often we try to hide these elements from others. Or, like many of us, you could be playing the role of the victim and continually presenting your wounds to the world.

If we have not been cherished in our upbringing then we do not understand at a deep level what it really means to love our self. Our measure of self-worth then comes from external sources. We take on the values of our peers and society as a measure of who we are, and because of this we are forever at their mercy. Looking for self this way means that we will never have a positive picture of ourselves that is foundational.

Without a positive view of who we are, we accumulate more and more stress as we grow older. In time this can result in us becoming vulnerable to illness. When we face our pain and go through it, we begin to grow emotionally as well as spiritually.

As we accumulate stress we begin to see less beauty in the world. During my time learning Transcendental Meditation (TM) my teachers sometimes referred to the Bliss State. About six weeks after I began TM, I walked outside after my morning meditation, and I saw that the sky was the most beautiful blue and the flowers vivid in colour, just the way I'd remembered them as a child.

When I told my teachers what I had experienced for most of that day, they explained that I had indeed enjoyed the Bliss State. I'd read somewhere that a child experiences this true view of the world's natural beauty more regularly than an adult does. This rang true with my memories.

When I was four I had my first experience of seeing the ocean. It's one of a few memories I have from that age, and I think I'm so lucky to recall them. We were at Lancelin, which in those days was six hours' drive north of Fremantle, along some rough bush tracks.

Dad had pitched a tent just back from the beach on the flat, behind the sand dunes. After we had breakfast on the first morning my eldest sister Nancy and I were allowed to go to the beach. Our two older cousins, whose father also worked at Lancelin, were charged with looking after us.

Because it was my first time, I was excited. But when the others quickly ran ahead of me I began to cry, because my legs couldn't keep up. Suddenly, I found myself alone in the dunes. I stopped, as a range of sensations washed over me. I was flooded with the warmth of the morning sun and the sound of cicadas as they beat out their clicking rhythm in the rising heat. A salty scent came to my nostrils; it was mixed with the aroma of coastal heath. Pigweed was growing everywhere in a display of the brightest pink flowers.

I was enthralled by what I could see, smell and hear. As I stood there I heard something. It was a subdued but powerful noise. I quickly worked my way through the dunes to find its source. When I reached the top I was overwhelmed by the beautiful blue waters of the Indian Ocean. I could see the bubbling foam of waves breaking on the outer reef. Brightly coloured fishing boats bobbed on their moorings and the white sandy beach stretched for miles in front of me.

I heard my sister shout, 'Come on!' and I ran towards her to embrace the adventure. As adults, how many of us still run to embrace the adventure? Most of us batten down the hatches and attempt to maintain the status quo, not realising that we are missing something wonderful—life.

What I've described as the Bliss State and the view of the child are basically the same thing. It is a true look at what life is really like when the mind is not cluttered with learned behaviour. As we grow into adulthood and accumulate stress (fear or pain) as a result of our resistance to the flow of life, our appreciation for life's beauty begins to lessen. But if we begin to confront the fears we have built over our lifetime, our view will begin to clear.

There is definitely a dissolving effect on fear when it is confronted with courage and a spirit of adventure. Like the child, once again we begin to find excitement in everyday things, as if we have discovered something wondrous for the first time. This clearing of our view generally doesn't take place overnight. Anything worthwhile usually takes time. It also takes a willingness to change and to grow, and it requires a desire to experience joy in our life rather than suffering.

As I said earlier, the pain I felt, particularly after my first marriage ended, was grief for the family I'd lost. The real depth of my depression came about because I lived my entire life in the physical world. I had no connection or foundation with anything greater than myself. You can call this power 'God', 'life', or whatever you are comfortable with. To my mind it is a First Cause, irrespective of any religion. But break its laws and you will feel the pain of life.

Back then I thought that achievement in life was the result of individual effort. It was only amid the darkness of my deepest suffering that I began to get in touch with this First Cause. If I had been told of this universal power through religion, I'm certain I would have rejected it because of my childhood experiences with the church. Fortunately for me, the books I read were presented in a scientific and spiritual way, an approach that I embraced.

Some have accused me of being religious, as if that is something terrible. In the past I may have joined in their chorus, and pointed my finger at those who practised any kind of faith. But now I know better. I follow no religion, even though I was christened a Catholic. The more I encountered quotes from the holy books of the world, the more wisdom I discovered in them. I have respect for all religions, as long as they promote and practise wisdom and love for others.

For me, my faith in this intelligence has come from my own personal day-to-day struggle with life. It is through understanding the rules that I experienced a deeper connection with life than I'd been able to achieve before. I realised that money alone wouldn't do it for me, nor would alcohol or sex. I demanded more satisfaction from life than I'd previously experienced.

My practise of meditation helped me greatly in furthering my connection with life. I feel meditation is really a deeper form of prayer that assists this connection. It didn't shift my thinking overnight; it was more a gradual and subtle change. Now I don't flinch at that word 'God' as I did when I picked up my first Louise Hay book all those years ago.

There is something Dr Wayne Dyer talks about in his audiotape *There's a Spiritual Solution to Every Problem* that has come to be true for me. He advocates that we need to gain personal experience of God to nurture faith in Him. For me it happened with the results of my first back affirmation, but it doesn't have to be that dramatic. The gradual building of trust will develop your foundation of faith. Once you begin on this path, faith will grow stronger within you. You will feel more supported as you relate to life from a spiritual perspective.

The art of meditation can be a vehicle for bringing peace into your day-to-day life. In the West there is still some resistance to it. I think from certain aspects it is a cultural fear because of the unknown (resistance to the flow of life). This is always driven by the ego, which would have us believe that we operate purely as individuals without connection to anything beyond the physical.

It's this fear that stops us thinking deeply about life. Because if we did, we would not only discover that there is an intelligence that created the universe but that it continues to operate in a very ordered way. We know that over time meditation is an effective way of dissolving one's fears. Each time we overcome a fear we're able to further embrace life.

Some people have concerns about meditation. They're afraid they may be sucked into an unscrupulous cult or religion. As with all things in life, you will have to use your commonsense, if and when you decide to get involved. Meditation is not a religion of any type. Some religions practise it, but more than anything, it is a way of achieving clarity and peace of mind. The fact is you may learn a classical meditation without getting involved in any religion or organisation.

After I spent a number of years developing my meditation skills I decided to add visualisations to the end of my sessions. This tied in well with my study and practise of metaphysics. Remember, what you think and see clearly in your mind, on an ongoing basis, will manifest in your life. I've found that at the end of a meditation the mind is calmer and more receptive to a visualisation. What this means is that the picture you create will penetrate deeper into your subconscious mind, and will more quickly become part of your everyday thinking. After a while I started to experience some of my visualisations in my physical life.

For those who say they don't have time to meditate, you simply need to get up half an hour earlier in the morning. Ideally you should also meditate in the late afternoon or early evening. In the end, if you really want to make some changes in your life, you'll find a way to do it.

An average meditation practice will consist of 20 to 30 minutes twice a day. The early morning session works well directly after exercise because the mind is stimulated by physical activity. Studies have shown that this creates better quality meditations. It's wise not to listen to the news or read the papers before you meditate in the morning. Once you've completed your session then it's fine to catch up with these things. Listening to the news once or twice a day is okay to keep yourself informed about what's going on in the world, but any more than that and you begin to overdose. The reason is that most of what we see or hear on the news is negative, and therefore constant exposure to it increases the stress in our lives.

Afternoon or evening practice will help dissolve accumulated stress from the day, as well as long-term stress. Don't judge your individual sessions for quality, or your overall practice for that matter. It's much like a life review. Six or 12 months' time gives a clearer picture of how you are going. Just know that many wise people throughout history have confirmed that meditation works. They speak of a growing calmness within, and a peace and appreciation for life that will expand as you practise. This is nothing to be afraid of but rather something to look forward to.

Meditation, however, is not the only way to relax the mind. Sitting still for 20 to 30 minutes will also have a calming effect; this is better done with the eyes closed. After about 15 minutes you will find that tranquillity begins to settle in your mind.

There are still further ways to achieve peace of mind. Sitting or walking quietly in a forest or by the ocean can achieve similar results. Listening to certain types of music will also unburden the mind (classical works well). Reading about the meaning of life is greatly healing as well. This type of literature widens our perspective on life, as well as deepening our connection with it.

All of this is best done in a quiet setting so that the mind has the opportunity to release its accumulated stress. As the process takes place, it allows solutions to our problems to come into consciousness. Here, awareness will pick them up, and put them to use in our life. The more you make this type of practice a regular part of your daily life, the more benefit you'll receive.

If you decide meditation is not for you, then that's fine. But I do think it's essential to practise allowing the mind to unwind each day. This doesn't include sitting and watching TV. You may think you are relaxing but in actual fact the mind is being bombarded by a great deal of negativity, which only serves to increase our stress.

As I have already mentioned, the news is a perfect example of concentrating almost exclusively on the negative actions in the world. The problem with this is that it gives us a skewed view of what the world is really like. Violence in movies is another way of desensitising us to the connection we have with each other. Overexposure to this type of information in the long term will make us less compassionate towards all of life. For a percentage of people it can result in violent behaviour.

It's up to us to choose the things that nourish us. This ranges from the food we eat to the people we associate with, right through to what we choose to watch and read. Most importantly, we need to become aware of the thoughts we allow into our minds. By becoming aware, and directing our thoughts, we can influence the direction our life takes. Then, like the child, we will recognise adventure and embrace it.

4

Action

THE WORD 'ACTION' often causes some confusion when it is used in the context of healing a life. What does action really mean? Some would say it is a physical deed, or making a decision to change. Still others would suggest it is a spiritual transformation. In fact, it is all of these things and more.

If we want to grow, this certainly means we need to grow spiritually. To grow we have to take action through our heart. When we act via our heart it means we are less inclined to take actions that are based on fear. As with all things in life, action needs to be balanced. If someone is about to physically harm us it's no good thinking loving thoughts at that very moment. We need either to take action to protect ourselves or remove ourselves from the situation.

In developed societies, we tend to believe that intellectual thought, coupled with technology and materialism, will bring us the things we desire. Yet as many of us reach these deeply desired goals, we find an emptiness that often leaves us bewildered. The current generation has much more material wealth than previous generations, and yet they are spiritually less happy than were their parents and grandparents.

I experienced some of what today's society is suffering when I was lobster fishing. Right when I reached my highest level of income, and was finally earning the kind of money I had desired, I felt less joy than at any point in my life. Some might say that was because my marriage had just broken up, and I was alone. This is a valid point, and it had much to do with my unhappiness at the time—but it was also only part of the reason why I felt that way.

To think that I have something against wealth would be to misunderstand me. I believe that having monetary wealth is a good thing—but *only* if it is not at the expense of your spiritual self, or to the detriment of others. To earn a lot of money and grow personally, as well as spiritually, is a wonderful expression of life in action.

Great wealth becomes even more valuable if you use it to help others. This wealth can assist the less advantaged to achieve better lives through things like education and specialised mentor programs. Using personal riches this way provides a great service to the world.

When we give in this way, we feel energised and self-empowered. If your intention is truly to help others grow, and not just to look for accolades, then both you and the one you're helping will feel expanded, and greater than you were before. By taking action this way you will prosper through the compound effect of giving. Once again, this is about the flow of energy.

For those whose only goal it is to earn a lot of money for personal wealth accumulation and power over others, there is eventually a price to pay. It is the price of emptiness and aloneness. There are many examples throughout history of wealthy people who were deeply unhappy. Without the higher goal of helping others, the accumulation of wealth is much like a drug addiction. One is driven by an ever-increasing need to increase income and to collect things.

During my years of fishing, I was taking action in the world and wondering why that action wasn't bringing me the happiness I expected. I now know that it was because my reason for earning money was driven by my fear of poverty, and not by a higher purpose.

It was this attitude that created a lack of balance in my life. If anyone had suggested the world might have a spiritual dimension, I would've looked at him or her with my usual smugness. My security in life came from my higher income, and the increasing capital value of my business. This is where I sourced my power from in the world. But despite my conceit, I was fully aware that deep inside I was terrified. I continued this charade well into my forties, until life forced me to change.

How do we change our source of power from outside—in things, or others' opinions—to inside, where our true centre is? When we're able to do this we connect with the source of all life, the same source that governs the universe.

Life was trying to guide me gently in the right direction before I ever made the conscious choice to change, but did I take any notice? No—my intention was to marry, have children, earn a lot of money and retire by the age of 40. Other than wanting to be wealthy and have a happy family life I had no other goals. I hadn't thought much about the wider questions of life: why I was here, let alone whether I was here for a reason.

Occasionally I wondered if there was something else I should be doing. Could I have achieved more with my life—especially if I'd gotten an education? But I would always answer these questions by saying that when I had enough money I could do what I liked. I justified this by telling myself the money was necessary to protect me from the awful things that could happen in the world. I believed that money could solve most problems, except for maybe a serious illness, and of course, death. So to my mind, money would provide a solution to almost all the problems that might arise. From one angle this is true, but not when we look at a balanced life.

Interestingly it was only after I began to lose my assets, and had been seriously ill for some years, that this belief was challenged. Life has a curious way of making us face reality. At this point we can either choose to change and grow, or continue to suffer. Unfortunately, many of us continue to suffer. We do so because we believe it is more painful and frightening to change than it is to remain the same. The truth is that an unwillingness to change leads to much greater pain. This pain can continue until the day we die.

My new awareness didn't occur overnight. As this awakening tried to establish itself, my belief system fought it with all its might. It tried incredibly hard to keep the status quo, to continue doing what it had previously known. This is why the familiar always seems so safe; yet, the familiar can be a subtle, undetectable poison—inside, we know that we really are capable of achieving great things. It's only the layers of our learned fears that stop us from fulfilling this potential.

The problem for most of us is that we don't know we've been in jail for much of our lives, and that the jailer is our own belief system. When a particular fear is pointed out to an individual, in many cases they will deny being afraid. It is usually when one recognises that they are afraid that they are more likely to confront those fears, and eventually leave them behind.

The taking of action on any level is not easy, in fact, I can promise you that it will be hard, but in between those hard times some amazing things will occur. It's these in-between times that will inspire you onwards. This is when you'll be fully conscious of having moved another step towards freedom. It's quite exhilarating and yet humbling at the same time.

One area in which we can grow is in helping others. This is one of the greatest gifts we can give. I was a more selfish person 20 years ago, compared to my willingness to help others now, yet this was not planned. It came about because I wanted to heal my back injury and to calm my anxiety-ridden nervous system.

My empathy and compassion for others grew slowly over time as I read books of wisdom and established a practice of meditation. At first, I couldn't understand why people would go so far in helping others. I thought, yes, that's okay—but what's in it for them? Because at the same time it seemed some of these people were being used up.

When I was a child attending religious classes and church, I never fully appreciated some of the words of wisdom I heard, such as, 'You will always reap what you sow'. I had some understanding in the physical sense as to how this might work, but no idea that it might possibly relate to thought, and that thought was in effect energy which could manifest on the physical plane.

I do recall thinking at the time that there might be a white-bearded god up there. And I was afraid if I thought a bad thought, a bolt of lightning was coming my way—ah, those fire and brimstone days.

I can't tell you the exact day I began to change, that's how inconspicuous the process was for me, and yet for others, it can be dramatic. What I can say is that the taking of action in the areas of education, exercise, food and meditation slowly brought about this change in me. Once established, it's a path you can't turn away from easily. It will probably be the best habit you ever develop.

In my first few years of meditating I would sometimes become frustrated and stop practising for a while. This was when it seemed like I wasn't healing fast enough. I'd use this time to watch more television, eat extra food, and forget about exercise. After a while, something interesting began to happen. I found I began to miss the sanctuary of meditation. It brought me a feeling of peace and a greater connection to life.

There is a strong desire in me (I believe it is my purpose) to teach others how to break free of the shackles that keep them stuck. I want them to become conscious of the fears that stop them fully experiencing and appreciating life. When they get to this point they will be in a position to fulfil their destiny.

There is something very predictable about fear when it's challenged—it begins to dissolve. This has the effect of increasing one's courage, and therefore one's self-belief. When you look back over the years you'll be amazed at how far you have come.

As I continue on my journey of personal and spiritual development, I find that I think less and less about the past. It's common for some people who are stuck in their lives to think and talk often about the past. This longing is the thing that keeps them trapped. The view is that there is nothing exciting in the now, and even less to look forward to in the future.

If we start to take on new activities in the areas I've suggested, over time our preoccupation with the past will begin to lessen. We'll come to look over our history with a certain fondness, rather than wanting to relive it all the time—because the reality is we can never go back. The most fundamental thing about life is that it wants us to go forward and grow. Going back is not an option.

During the years when I was bedridden, I completed external study courses with two different adult colleges, but I often wondered where it was leading me. Even though I knew my literacy levels were improving, I just couldn't see how it was going to change my life significantly. Of course, I understood that better literacy would assist me in my day-to-day living, but I was unable to visualise a changed life in the future.

This once again shows how subtle healing can be. It was only with the wisdom of time that I recognised change had occurred. Usually this was when I would attempt to do something new and I found I could do it with relative ease. With the benefit of hindsight I understood it was because of some skill I'd picked up in an earlier course, or a program I'd learnt on my computer.

Often my knowledge was gained from books written by some of the world's great thinkers. I can't recall anything new that I took on which didn't benefit me in some way, even if I only learnt one small thing from each experience. The result would always be that I gained in knowledge, skill and wisdom. This is the way we grow.

In my quest to overcome back pain I discovered a book called *Healing Back Pain* written by John E. Sarno, M.D. The information in this book was one of the things that helped me take a major step forward in healing my lower back and sciatic pain.

Sarno suggested that back pain could be healed without surgery, drugs or exercise. He maintained that lower back and some other types of pain were caused by TMS (tension myositis syndrome). Essentially, this is tension held in the muscle. In his later book he goes on to say that not only is tension held in the muscles but also anywhere blood is supplied in the body.

The reason for the pain was oxygen deprivation. It took him some years to realise this was being orchestrated by the brain, specifically, the subconscious mind. Sarno's logic was that the subconscious was creating the pain as a diversion from the real issue of suppressed emotions.

The subconscious does this in certain personality types, because if these emotions were allowed to come to consciousness it would be unacceptable to that type of personality. The perfectionist is one of the personalities that is particularly susceptible. But in my experience I believe the subconscious plays a role in the majority of illnesses, in all personality types. Sarno tells us the suppressed emotion behind illness is rage. The subconscious fears that it would be unacceptable to express these emotions in public—hence the diversion of pain.

I certainly had the profile of a perfectionist and I'd never liked expressing my emotions. This was probably because my father was a highly emotional man and could explode easily in public. Somewhere along the way I'd decided it was better to keep quiet and not display my true feelings. Like many of us I also found it hard to handle angry people.

Expressing anger in appropriate ways is something I'm still in the process of learning about. In the end I think it comes down to educating yourself as much as you can about communication. The better you are at communicating, the more smoothly your life will run. But with other people, it is often simpler than this. You just need to step back and let them blow off steam.

The thing I liked about Sarno's approach to pain was its scientific basis. It was this view that helped me to further understand the metaphysical philosophy of life. The other thing that made healing easier was that I didn't have to discover the psychological cause before any healing could take place. Although finding the psychological cause is important, it is not imperative.

Sarno advises that if you are in pain, consult your doctor to make sure you have no life-threatening illness. Once you are cleared of anything life-threatening, you can begin. I must add that even if you do have something seriously wrong, a positive approach to healing would be a strong complement to any treatment you might receive. The power and strength of your mind cannot be underestimated.

There are many proven stories of people who have faced and overcome terrible health predictions. When these people are studied it is often found that they made great changes in their lives. As well as creating a powerful attitude of overcoming, most developed a more spiritual approach to their life.

One has to face one's fears. This is emphasised in books of wisdom throughout the ages. I found this was the hardest part. Sarno, too, says something similar. In the case of physical pain he suggested one had to do the very thing that caused that particular pain. This would be hard for most of us to accept because anything that causes pain automatically generates fear.

Some treatments instruct us to avoid particular activities that cause pain. I believe in many cases (but not all) that this can keep us stuck. For me, Sarno's approach meant that when I experienced pain sitting, I should deliberately go ahead and sit. Walking, bending or lifting was also agony for me—how was I going to confront those situations? And compounding these problems were my high anxiety levels. This left me with a whole range of things I had to work on. In the end I decided to start with lower back pain first, as well as some general anxieties.

On my first morning I drove five minutes to the Swan River where there are some scenic, relaxing walk paths. Up to this point the farthest I could walk was about 200 metres and that was normally very painful. As I slowly started to walk, I kept my mind alert for habitual thoughts that the subconscious would slip into my conscious mind. One has to be alert because this can take only a fraction of a second. If you aren't looking for this to happen, all you will be aware of is that you were suddenly thinking this thought.

The subconscious activates this as part of a standard and continuous 'movie' it plays—in fact it is the movie of your life. This film is rarely based on reality but it is a movie that you believe with all your heart to be true. Yes, that's right, you are convinced of something that has little or no truth to it. It is exactly what the subconscious wants you to believe.

When I first heard this it made a lot of sense to me because I knew we had all formed most of our opinions in childhood. And I understood that our emotions were driven by our world view, which was given to us by the dominant adults during our infancy and childhood.

Problems occur when the world doesn't conform to our view; strong emotional reactions flare within us. Because these reactions are not generally acceptable to display in public, the mind immediately suppresses them. As this happens many times over the ensuing years this suppression builds inside us and becomes accumulated stress. When this threatens to spill into consciousness the subconscious goes to work and creates a pain diversion.

What complicated creatures we are! Yet history shows for those of us who are willing to face our fears on an ongoing basis, emotional and physical pain can not only be decreased but actually healed. Life makes it very clear. For us to grow, we must face the challenges that confront us, because that is the key to wisdom and freedom.

It seems to me that there is a plan on a grand scale within the universe. I also believe within that plan there is an exciting chart for our individual destiny. If we could but catch a glimpse of what is possible for us we would never settle for mediocrity. Making the choice to settle for less is what creates the pain we experience in life.

So if the subconscious was playing a fictitious movie about a bad back, to divert me from being aware of suppressed emotions, it made a lot of sense. You see, I had come to believe that my movie was true in every way.

All my studies suggested the most sensible thing to do would be to rewrite the movie script and create a different film. But remember, this is your life script, and it has been well accepted by you for a long time, so it won't change overnight. Your role in the new movie must involve affirmations, visualisations, faith and facing fears—and yes, you get to play the hero. You can also include meditation if you so choose.

All of these are powerful weapons that can aid you in the battle ahead. Remember, you are never alone. When you can't find the strength you need to overcome a situation, just ask for help from life. Once you begin to look for this help it's interesting how the means to overcome the problem always seems to materialise.

I found I didn't have to take up a religion or meditate on a mountaintop for this help to become available to me. It was always there, but I discovered it never worked unless I played my part by taking action on the various levels.

When I began my walk, I would have rated my back pain as being four on a scale of one to ten. Just as I approached my normal limit of 200 metres I suddenly caught my subconscious mind in the process of tricking me. By this, I mean as I was beginning to take my next step, a picture of me with increasing back pain slipped almost unseen into my conscious mind. Within a few seconds my back pain had increased to a level of seven.

Sarno was absolutely right with his theory! I was aware that for the subconscious strategy to be effective it would have to be presented in picture form to be believed. These pictures are always negative and usually designed to restrict us in some way. They always cause pain, which is the perfect diversion for the brain's purpose.

It seemed sensible to me that this constant replay would, in time, manifest itself in the body just as the pictures represented. The level of pain would be proportionate to our belief in the pictures in our mind. The description I'd seen of myself suffering further pain occurred just before there was any actual increase in pain. It was a scene that had been replayed many times in the preceding years.

To me it was clear evidence that the picture (the natural process of thought becoming an image) created the physical response. It was also obvious that I could practise skills to create new pictures in my mind. By using these skills and confronting our fears we can heal our pain. Always remember to encourage and support your self as you go about the task.

Wouldn't it be great if our minds were just like a video or a DVD? We could wipe the old pictures out and then copy the new movie we wanted straight over the top. In fact we are doing something very similar with the methods I've suggested in this book. Rather than wiping our minds clean we are recording over the top. We are doing this by repeating affirmations and working on our visualisations, then taking physical action to back up those mental deeds and images. Once the new suggestions have become habit we have successfully 'recorded over' the old belief.

Occasionally old beliefs may resurface when we're under pressure but with a little perseverance the new habits will reassert themselves.

I think there is a good reason for us not generally being able to change our view of the world quickly. It has to do with spiritual development. This is happening on a world scale and at the same time on an individual level. Spiritual consciousness will take time. How long? I can't tell you. But I do feel, as do many others in the world today, that it is happening at a faster rate than previously. We can increase this forward momentum. What we do as individuals has an effect on the world as we choose to take responsibility for our own maturity.

With my pain increasing, the pictures were coming more quickly and vividly. There were ones of me in great agony. Another flashed into my mind of being stuck by the roadside unable to move or drive my car home. With each new and frightening view the pain became more intense.

Further pictures flashed into my mind about discs protruding into my sciatic nerve. I saw myself at an appointment with the head of neurosurgery at the hospital where I was operated on. He was telling me that the scar tissue damage to my sciatic nerve was too severe to allow further surgery. By now the pain had moved up to ten out of ten. I started to worry that I might be doing myself further damage—but still I continued.

In the middle of the pain I began to work on positive affirmations of a strong healthy back, although I found it hard to believe them. Affirmations are great, but when you're in the middle of that sort of pain it's not easy to remain calm.

Suddenly my mind became distracted by the beautiful view of the river. It was glassy, and flowing along at a lazy pace in the still morning air. Just when I thought I couldn't stand the pain any longer it backed off a little. I realised that as I looked at the river the thought of how beautiful it was had replaced the picture of pain in my mind. This is the way thought manifests and then affects the body. One pleasant picture lasting 30 seconds was enough to reduce my level of pain to a seven.

That day I walked just over half a kilometre for the first time in more than two years. The next day the distance increased to one kilometre. Within three months I was covering up to five kilometres.

Although I was often in considerable pain, there were moments when I was able to shift my mind to more pleasant things. When I was successful, my pain levels would drop within seconds. As this was happening I came to realise how powerful the mind really is. It became increasingly apparent to me that as individuals we need to become more conscious and take control of how we use our minds.

Even though healing never came that quickly for me I did experience occasional relief, which supported my belief in following this new road. I guessed I was on the road that Robert Frost spoke of—the one 'less travelled'.

There were many times, especially over the following three years, when I thought I was kidding myself about healing my back pain. Memories of what medical authorities had told me to expect were deep in my mind.

The thing I disliked most about the medical approach was the general lack of hope it gave me. Before any procedure I would be told about all its possible side effects. Being informed about these was fair enough. I think that what annoyed me most was that there was little enthusiasm for what could go right, or the probability of healing.

Despite this experience I had to be careful not to become pessimistic. I needed to remind myself that there were good people with great skill in the medical profession. I tried to remember that I shouldn't discount them all because some were indifferent or lacked compassion.

Whenever I was ill I measured my intention to heal myself against the likelihood of needing medical help. The way I did this was to ask: could this be TMS (tension myositis syndrome), in other words, emotionally driven? I believe most illnesses are initiated by an emotional state. Even the contraction of viruses comes down to how healthy your entire immune system is. A person with good mental health will tend to have good emotional health because they view things in balance. When coupled with exercise and a healthy diet, the possibility of illness is reduced.

Sometimes, even when the medical evidence said I needed to undergo a certain treatment or procedure, I would not go ahead. I'm not recommending that you do this. But before I ever made that decision I would evaluate all the medical evidence. When doing this I had no intention of putting my life or health in any danger. If I was satisfied, the next step was to check out any emotional issues and work on those.

So as you can see, there is a range of actions we can take. But the most important action is to begin to take control of our minds, specifically, our thoughts. If we don't understand this vital point then we will spend our time reacting to the winds and tides of life, rather than setting our course for our chosen destination.

5

Stay the Path

If you asked me how I overcame pain despite the negative medical outlook, I would tell you that I applied two crucial things—persistence and faith. When one studies any success story both these attitudes will be present.

I would like to clarify my use of the word 'success' as meaning lasting success. So-called instant prosperity in any field generally disappears as fast as it comes. Lasting achievement only materialises after the essential foundations have been laid. This takes time and effort. If you aren't prepared to put consistent effort into changing your life then any success you achieve may well be short-lived.

Often in the middle of trying to overcome pain or a difficult life situation, I would decide it was all too hard. But further consideration made me realise the alternative was much worse. I knew that to shrink from change and return to the way things were was really no choice at all. This is because going back is generally the cause of the problem. Pain of any description is life's way of telling us that what we are doing is not working and we must change it.

So what do we do when a situation seems too difficult to solve, even though we may have asked the universe for help and it hasn't arrived? The answer is quite simple—have faith. Growing up, I'd always had a dogged characteristic to my personality. It was this trait that helped me gain momentum at the start of my new spiritual journey. But it was the development of faith that created a true persistence.

As we grow in faith we must also be careful not to become inflexible in our attitudes towards our goal, as this can eventually leave us feeling isolated and burdened. We may start to believe that we have to achieve everything on our own. If this attitude prevails we may find that little, if any, help arrives to solve our problem.

With ongoing practice I discovered if I took action towards a goal and relinquished my driving attitude, and just trusted life, things began to work out as if they were following some magical plan.

All my life I had worked hard but never trusted life. It was such a wonderful surprise to discover that there was an intelligent order to the way life worked. My success with affirmations and the gradual giving up of control allowed me to develop a faith that didn't exist before. I decided to devote myself to developing deeper levels of faith for the rest of my life. I knew it would not be an easy job but I decided to make this my aim as I went about my everyday tasks.

In his book, John Sarno suggests that when one confronts pain (fear) the subconscious will at some point give up creating that pain. In the case of physical pain, how much we fear taking part in the activity determines and perpetuates that distress. It is also our level of fear that governs the intensity of the pain. What a catch-22 situation; we are truly our own worst enemy.

Remember, confronting fear is best done gently. This means we don't start with an activity that causes enormous discomfort. We begin by dealing with the lower levels of pain so we might gain our mental and physical confidence.

In my case, I decided to avoid lifting and instead worked on being able to sit with comfort again after years of being bedridden. I didn't really care at my age if I wasn't able to lift heavy weights again. But I wanted to be able to sit and enjoy a range of normal activities. Even though medical specialists advised me to avoid sitting for long periods because of disc protrusions I thought it was time for me to confront this belief. When I say 'belief' I mean that not only was it the accepted medical belief but also my own.

Like the majority of us I was brought up to respect people in authority. So if a doctor gave a medical opinion I tended to accept it at the conscious and subconscious level, whether it was right or wrong.

One day I decided to go to the movies. I prepared by arming myself with some heavy-duty painkillers. Sitting in a theatre was something I hadn't been able to do for three years or so. Even prior to that time it had been a painful exercise, and therefore never an enjoyable experience. This only served to increase my anger and resentment because I really liked the movies. It was just another thing that I saw life had taken away from me. I decided to confront this pain situation even though I was very much afraid of it.

Half an hour before leaving for the movies I took a painkiller and put another in my pocket, just in case. The ten-minute drive to the theatre was enough time for my mind to develop numerous horror scenarios of back pain. I saw scenes of myself being stuck in the seat at the theatre with emergency services working on me. When these pictures appeared I ignored them as best I could, whilst working on positive affirmations. My only hope was that the affirmations would sink into my subconscious and have a counteracting effect on the fearful images I was experiencing.

Going to the movies alone never inspired me; it just reminded me that I didn't have a partner any more. But this day I didn't care, as I was going to beat this thing called pain. The movie I chose was *Gladiator*. It played for approximately three hours and it was the longest-running movie at the time. I had decided to really test Sarno's theory. By the time I took my seat in the theatre, sweat beads were forming on my brow and upper lip.

Everything I learnt from meditation and books of wisdom told me that I had to take my attention away from the pain. When we experience any type of pain our attention is well and truly focused on the discomfort, and not in the present moment, where it should be. It is this shift of attention that will mean the difference between suffering and freedom. This shift not only relates to pain but also encompasses the way we experience every part of life. It colours our opinions on subjects ranging from happiness through to money and relationships.

If you're enjoying a beautiful spring morning by noticing the amazing colours of all the flowers, and the blueness of the sky, and if you're breathing in the different scents around you, then you can bet your attention is fully on the beauty of the present moment. But if you get up on a morning that is superb and all you feel is despair, then you can be sure your mind is on your worries. It is our mind that gives us our experience of the world. Whether it is money or pain it all has to do with our view, which then goes on to create our experience of the situation.

Robert T. Kiyosaki indicates in his book *Rich Dad Poor Dad* that if we want to be rich we shouldn't work hard for money or worry about it. Yet the prevailing view in society is the very opposite. This is an indication of why so many people struggle with money. Those who take Kiyosaki's approach tend to spend less time worrying about money. This frees up their minds to develop ideas about generating more income. At the same time it makes it easier for them to recognise opportunities when they present themselves in their lives.

For example, you can have very opposite outcomes from two people winning the same amount of money in a lottery. One person begins to worry about what they will do with it all. Then there are concerns over making a mistake and losing it. Not to mention the relationship problems that might arise if they don't give some money to certain people, or the expected amount.

The other winner's mind is filled with all the things they can now buy and the family and friends they will be able to help. They're so excited about the overseas holiday they thought would never happen.

At the same time they're getting professional advice on investments that they weren't able to take advantage of before.

These vastly different responses to the same situation will also determine the different levels of health for those individuals. When one comes to understand this, it then becomes clear that our perspective not only affects our health but our very happiness. I believe one of the reasons we are here is to experience happiness on a regular basis and to spread it to others through loving acts and thoughts. By practising this we tend to complete the circuit of positive energy in which everyone benefits from our actions as well as ourselves. What we do affects things on a personal level as well as at the global level.

A mind that is on its worries is far less joyful than a mind that is excited about the adventure ahead. It's up to you what direction your thoughts, and therefore your life, are heading in. So this day at the theatre it was my job to place my full attention on the movie—to immerse myself in every part of it. I was going to take the attitude that pain was a game that my mind was playing. It was a game I was determined to win.

Within a short while of sitting down, my pain levels began to escalate. It became so intense that I thought I was going to have to leave the theatre or be carried out, just as my frightening images had predicted. I quickly took a tablet of the same type I'd taken earlier but one that was faster-acting. My doctor had suggested that I do this if ever I experienced pain that I couldn't manage. Somehow I hung on for the 30 minutes in which time the tablet was supposed to work. As I waited I reminded myself of Sarno's theory about confronting pain. I hoped he was right.

I sat there for over an hour. It was then I realised that my mind was not fully on the movie. Playing in the background were the pictures of pain. I decided to stop all the positive affirmations I had been silently saying to myself. At the same time I quit checking my pain levels.

Some ten minutes later I found I was deeply engrossed in the movie. By the end of the movie my pain levels had dropped by 70 per cent. I knew it wasn't the tablets because they'd had more than enough time to work. To me it was a clear indication that the relief had come about because my mind had shifted its focus onto the movie. Yes! I felt like standing on the seat and shouting my discovery to the world.

I had a growing body of evidence now that I was not a victim of my illness. This evidence showed me that being ill had more to do with my thoughts rather than illness per se. I vowed to come back to watch other movies, to challenge the fear of the subconscious mind. My belief was growing that I could overcome my situation irrespective of the current medical and physical evidence.

I realised from my past experience that things might not move quickly for me. I also understood that thinking in those terms was also a belief—one that could be changed. A conviction started to grow inside me that no matter what, I would continue down this path because this was where the answers lay. Every time I came up against high levels of pain I had to remind myself of my new belief.

There is one thing about the path of healing which at some point always becomes true for everyone. It is the fact that no matter how dedicated you are, you can expect to meet setbacks. These setbacks can occur many times. In fact, it is the natural flow of life giving us a chance to overcome. By overcoming, we automatically become more than we previously were. In other words we transcend our fear and grow in wisdom.

Having faith in something greater than you can make the difference between giving up and succeeding. Once again, having faith does not mean that you have to become religious. All you need to do is understand that there is a force that will provide answers for you.

After meditating twice a day for 18 months I became bored and stopped practising for a while. I understood with an activity like meditation that it certainly had the ability to heal illness in the body, by way of calming the emotions and integrating them in a balanced way with the nervous system. This in turn would have a beneficial effect on the whole physiology.

There was an experience I wasn't quite ready for. It was a loving force that I started to encounter in my day-to-day life. I can only describe it this way because there was an increasing sense of joy and of being guided and comforted. When I stopped practising, this feeling of comfort would begin to disappear. As soon as I started again I would once more experience these feelings as well as a sense of support by something very gentle, yet powerful.

I've said earlier that there is more than one way to experience this type of support without having to meditate. I've read and heard about people who've never meditated and yet have encountered similar experiences. I've also felt the same calmness after reading books of wisdom.

There are those who devote their time to helping others who are suffering who speak of the same feelings. It's interesting how the giver of comfort can also experience feelings of joy and comfort. It is a result of connecting with each other at the spiritual level and reminds each of us of our true self.

The wonderful thing about meditation is that once you are taught it you can then carry on your own private practice, which will enhance your life in many ways. Another thing I've always liked about meditation is that answers to one's most pressing problems often emerge.

These answers don't necessarily come with clarity for the entire life journey ahead. More often the process simply reveals the next turn in the road. If I take action and head down that road, more answers are revealed to me. Remember that in the end it will take action in the physical world to resolve life situations as well as the action of thought.

I've found that if I ignore these answers it's not long before life presents me with another problem in the same area. Once again we are being given an opportunity to grow by overcoming. If we choose to ignore the opportunity we continue to suffer until we get the message. Some people remain stuck in this cycle of suffering for the rest of their lives, because it is too frightening to move forward. The solution always requires us to confront the situation, go through the pain and then move on. It is the action of going through the pain that does the healing; it is also here that the lesson is really learnt. Mostly we don't recognise this until we view the situation in retrospect.

As humans our first reaction is to avoid pain. I remember when automatic teller machines (ATMs) first came out. I went to the bank and picked up an instruction pamphlet so I could learn how to use one properly. Everything went fine for a few months until one day I made an error and didn't know how to correct my mistake. There was a queue behind me and I became embarrassed. The people waiting grew frustrated and in the end I cancelled my transaction and left. It so upset my confidence that I didn't use an ATM for more than a year.

During that time I needed to use an ATM on a number of occasions but I always avoided them, even though it would have been much more convenient for me to use one. Several times I ran short of money on a weekend and of course the banks weren't open. I was frustrated; I knew somehow that I had to overcome my fear. So what did I have to do? Yes, that's right, go through my fear and learn to use ATMs in front of others, embarrassed or not.

From that point on, instead of ATMs causing me fear they became a kind of game. Because of this I became much more relaxed when using them. For a while I was always on the lookout for new terminals so I could see how different ones operated.

It's amazing how many elderly people have resisted using ATMs because of the fear of the new. Even though this example might appear to be a minor issue to some, it's actually very frightening to those suffering from the fear. There is an incredible range of things we, as humans, are afraid of. On their own, some of these fears may be slight but when combined with other fears they become the shackles that bind us. Each time we let fear stop us from doing something a little more of our freedom is lost.

Another experience I had with meditation was that my eyes began to well up during each practice and the occasional tear would fall. This went on for over two years. It was a sadness that seemed to come from deep within my heart. When I asked my teacher about this she suggested that it might be a release of accumulated stress. I had to agree with her because that's exactly what it felt like.

Even though I wasn't experiencing sad thoughts when this was happening, it's an example of what can be driving us at the subconscious level. There are many layers to the mind and this instance shows how meditation can penetrate its depths and release stress. The process frees us from our conscious intellectual mind and allows us truly to unwind.

It's also important for us to begin to take control of the conscious mind. If we do not apply some discipline, the mind will run off in numerous directions. It's this running off that causes an overreaction of the emotions. When the mind is allowed to do this it wastes our precious energy.

It is the persistence of positive affirming statements about your self, backed up by visualisations, that will eventually influence the deeper levels of your mind. In addition, when you take physical action in alignment with those statements you will be—perhaps for the first time—taking control of the direction of your life.

When I was younger I didn't have the resilience that I have today. I always thought that resilience meant being tough physically. My understanding became clearer after I'd studied books of wisdom and meditated for a few years. Resilience has more to do with understanding the natural flow of life. As a young man I spent much of my time going against the flow, and that really came from not trusting the process of life itself. Resilience is about knowing that when you have missed an opportunity another one will come your way and you will be better prepared for it next time.

I understood even more about resilience when I began to read about people who overcame severe illness or great adversity in their lives. Those who helped others in an unselfish way also inspired me; this included great spiritual leaders. Often when I studied their stories I would find they went through considerable suffering. But with persistence and faith, in either themselves or something greater, they went on to overcome and succeed.

So it is clear that if you want to accomplish whatever you're aiming for, you must persist. To do this I believe you need to develop some kind of faith or belief beyond yourself. Having a belief in something greater gives us strength in those times when we're overwhelmed by difficult life situations.

A short while after I first injured my back I began physiotherapy. The people who set up my program were experts. In me they had a willing student. I studied the exercises carefully and never missed a session, but in the end I didn't improve; in fact, I actually deteriorated. I finished up with the same result after several programs. There was nothing wrong with the people treating me, or with the exercises themselves.

When I eventually gave up on the physiotherapists I set about designing my own program after having read several books on the subject of lower back injuries. Some 18 months later I had to admit that my results were no better. The only difference was that my program was free.

One benefit of my reading was that I became aware of the advantages of stretching. Stretching will give you great flexibility throughout your life—especially in old age. If combined with some regular walking in tranquil settings you will discover your energy levels will be consistently higher. People in their seventies who apply this find they often have better flexibility and health than many people in middle age—particularly those who overindulge and don't exercise.

As I write this book it's only with the advantage of experience and hindsight that I can understand what was happening to me at the time. I applied persistence in everything I did, especially the exercises. Affirmations had become a natural part of my life. I repeated hundreds to myself every day, most of them silently. I didn't agree with the over-the-top and out-there approach of shouting them out to the world. I'm sure it's successful for some but it didn't suit my shy nature.

Visualisations were something I was still working on. I had difficulty seeing myself as healthy, happy and prosperous. Even though I saw my inability to visualise as a problem, it didn't seem to be the main cause of my lack of progress.

Increasing the rate of my progress required something more than the persistence I had already applied. If I wanted to overcome my situation and create a happy life I had to find the answer. That 'something more' turned out to be two things. Even though I was taking action to heal my back injury I wasn't really taking enough action to get myself working and to create an income. Often I would tell myself that study would lead me to where I wanted to go. While that thinking was correct to some extent, I also needed some part-time work to assist me with my income. My problem was that I wasn't able to do much at all.

It was around this time that I ran into an old friend who told me about the exchange-traded options market. It sounded good to me: finally an opportunity to earn some income again, but it was risky. Even so, I was desperate, and I wanted to fight my way out of the situation I found myself in, rather than go meekly into bankruptcy.

Before I could invest, I had to sell my home to raise some money. My wife was against the idea; needless to say this didn't help our marriage. But even without this extra conflict our marriage would not have survived because we didn't have the skills to work together as a loving couple. The disharmony we were experiencing was a reflection of our fears and our level of emotional maturity.

Initially I had great success investing in the options market. This, however, didn't last for very long. My profits began to turn to losses.

My anxiety increased. The truth is, after four years of trading I didn't believe the options market was real investing. I felt it was just a group of people on either side of a contract *betting* which way a stock would move. Up or down? It didn't seem any different to me than other forms of gambling. I also felt that contract prices often weren't a true reflection of the state of the company or the quality of the people working in it.

I decided to invest directly into shares instead. I already owned some shares after being exercised into them (that is, forced by the other party in the contract to buy the shares) via some earlier options trades.

In the beginning I was excited about buying shares, but after some time passed I found the share market gave me a similar return to the options market. Over three years of share investing I saw more than half of my remaining savings disappear. Forty per cent of this was due to companies going bankrupt. The world 'bear' market (a slowly declining market over a long period) compounded my overall losses. This began in the year 2000 and went through to the beginning of 2003.

My situation was made even worse because the home I was renting was costing me more than 60 per cent of my pension. It wasn't particularly expensive—unless you were on a government pension. I had applied for state housing but there was a long waiting list. The problem as I saw it was that I didn't have enough capital left to recover my losses or, possibly, to survive financially. What a long way I'd fallen since the days of owning and operating my own lobster boat with its above-average income.

The attitude I developed towards options trading came out of a kind of emptiness with what I was doing. Even though I felt this, I didn't realise it stemmed from a lack of connection to real things. The problem was that I had no bond with, or any deep understanding of, the companies I was investing in. Some of financial icon Warren Buffet's comments, quoted in *Huntleys' Your Money Weekly*, a newsletter which I subscribed to at the time, helped me understand my feelings about options trading.

Buffet indicated that options placed unreal pressure on the value and performance of shares in a public company. In other words, traders would attempt to manipulate situations for their own reasons irrespective of how the company was running its business.

Manipulation has always gone on with share trading. But the options market allows a greater level of gearing (trading with a higher percentage of money than you actually have), compounding this problem. Therefore it can generate an even greater distortion of the share price. This practice not only affects companies but stock markets. At its worst it can cause undue pressure on a country's economy.

Much the same thing occurs in currency trading. Large funds can put great stress on a country's economy by driving the value of its currency down. Not much thought is given by these funds to the populations who suffer the after-effects of this kind of trading.

In recent times large corporations have become more heavily involved in options as a means of protecting their interests or to gain income. Buffet suggests the best thing they could do would be to focus on running their business well, and then the rest will naturally take care of itself.

In my own way I wanted to leave the herd mentality and become conscious about my investments. With my changing attitude I decided to be more selective in the companies I invested in. At the same time, I had no intention of transforming myself into a 'greenie', but I had a desire to become more aware of what I was investing in, for reasons beyond just making a quick dollar.

I went in search of good companies operated by quality people. Once I identified them I wanted to stay with them and give them my support like a good friend. I knew that in the long term they would reward me.

By October 2002 the world markets were at their lowest point in years. Bankruptcies were being reported almost weekly in the US and we were having our own problems in Australia, although not anywhere near to the same extent. My confidence was low, but deep inside there was a glimmer of belief that I could eventually be successful with my new approach.

What I can tell you is that my persistence led me to a more successful—and more relaxing—way of investing. But more importantly it was my growing faith that enabled me to stay the path. This was despite the constant shadow of bankruptcy that always hung over me.

6

Fear and Trust

FEAR AND TRUST affect every aspect of our lives. Often we are not aware that almost every decision we make is a choice out of fear or trust. Unfortunately fear tends to dominate in many of us. It is fear that stops us from reaching for our dreams or achieving our ambitions. Fear and trust could almost be described as the pessimist and the optimist within us.

I believe that fear comes from a lack of trust in one's inner self and, just as importantly, a lack of trust in the world. Of course this lack of trust generally reflects our view of life. Fear not only retards our growth as individuals but it can also affect nations and the world in a similar way.

Since the attack on the World Trade Center in the United States, international fear of Muslims has grown. Out of this tragedy a great anxiety has developed. 'Terror' has become the new threat, and the perceived threat, the fear of which quickly spread around the world. I believe some of the leaders in the western world, and most certainly the media, have magnified this fear, making it difficult to see the truth clearly.

I'm not talking here about what a government has to do to increase homeland security because of terrorism. The fear I'm describing is at the individual and public level. When fear of the other is magnified it also becomes distorted. At this point we stop perceiving the other as human. This distortion not only encompasses our fear of Muslims but also their fear of us. Go back in history and you'll find it includes any enemy's perception of the other. It can also take in fanatical religious views, racism and prejudice towards those who are different.

None of these outlooks are ever based on love; they are simply driven by *fear*. A difference in culture or religion is often the excuse to activate dormant fears. As I've said, this is even when the fear has no basis in reality.

Dr Harville Hendrix mentions something of this fear in his audio series, *Finding Love*. He talks about the chief of a tribe of cannibals, and about how the chief responds when asked how he could eat another human being? The chief's answer is that the enemy is not human! So from his perspective it is not only okay to kill the enemy—but also to eat him. He hasn't in any way conceived of his enemy as being a human being.

In the midst of our fear we can sometimes dehumanise the other. As with cultural fear we start to believe the so-called enemy is everywhere, and we cast a net of distrust over entire peoples or religions. We then sometimes go on to judge individuals by what we believe about that particular race or religion, whether it is true or not.

Rarely do we stop to consider that within a feared culture there are people with a humanitarian outlook. Neither would we think of them as loving parents. We also wouldn't allow ourselves to believe that they are *not* the enemy. If, for a moment, we admitted these things, the truth would be revealed. At that point we'd actually become conscious and our view of them as the enemy would be shattered.

I recall my father telling me about when he was drafted into the Australian Army during World War II. He spoke of the racism he experienced. I believe this was in part due to Italy initially supporting Adolf Hitler at the start of the war.

Even though my father was born in Fremantle, Western Australia, and his family had lived there since 1900, he was treated as if he was not an Australian. Some fearful individuals in the army and the community saw Italians as people not to be trusted. I can only imagine how Dad must have felt serving in the army of his country knowing that some Australians viewed him as some sort of enemy, or a breed not to be trusted.

When I began school in 1956, I understood a little of what my father had experienced. By the time I was ten I'd been in a number of fights after being racially abused. This attitude towards me continued until my early thirties. Even the fact that my mother was English made no difference. It seemed my olive skin and Italian surname were enough to attract trouble.

My father's experience derived from the same type of fear that dominates the world today—the fear of everything Muslim. In his own time, however, the fear happened to be of Italians. The attitude I encountered was predominantly the same, though to a lesser degree. I'm describing these situations only to highlight the fact that the driving force behind all of them can be distilled down to one thing—fear.

I recall the students in my school constantly criticising Italian food. Almost no-one I knew who was non-Italian ever ate it. Once again this is simply fear of the unknown. Now our cities are awash with Italian restaurants, and pizza seems to have been forever part of our culture. I'm sure if you closed all the pizza shops in Australia the teenagers in our society would be protesting in front of Parliament House. It's wonderful to see such a positive change emerge from a position of fear. The sad thing is that it took over half a century to resolve those fears.

The good thing is that fear, and this includes racism, is not inherent. It is environmentally taught and learnt. So not only do we as individuals have the opportunity to transform our lives by freeing ourselves of fear, but the world can evolve far more quickly if it too discards its generational and tribal fears. Almost all fears have little or no basis in reality. They are learnt as we grow and experience the world—but mostly they are passed down to us through the superstitions of generations before us.

As we evolve on our quest for personal and spiritual growth we become more conscious and discerning as to what we allow into our lives. This might range from the people we associate with to the books we read, how we use the internet, or the type of television we watch.

It is essential that we develop the skill of discernment to avoid polluting our minds with the negative thoughts of others. Some people believe that they can be regularly exposed to negative influences and still not be affected by that information. But research shows that our beliefs and actions are directly influenced by that exposure. In other words, the more mental rubbish we allow into our minds, the greater our beliefs are swayed by that information. This was revealed in some of my earliest studies of Brian Tracy. He confirms this from his own research and that of Dr David McClelland, of Harvard University.

In his audio series *The Psychology of Achievement*, Brian Tracy explains that someone can receive the very best training in personal growth, relationships and goal setting, but that in the end it can still have no long-term benefit. If the person still chooses to associate with a negative crowd that in itself is enough to ensure their failure. Maintaining negative links and absorbing negative information can turn us from being self-starters to self-doubters.

When my first marriage ended I found myself playing sad love songs and having constant thoughts of regret. I didn't understand at the time that at a subconscious level this was increasing my depression.

After my second marriage broke up I took a different attitude. Not only did I have to deal with being alone, but I was in extreme pain due to my unsuccessful back surgery. Taking care of myself was difficult. My new attitude included not entertaining negative thoughts.

Whenever I became conscious of my thoughts taking a negative direction I would work at changing them to positive thoughts.

I spent some of my time looking to connect with others. The type of people I chose were empathetic to my plight, but at the same time they didn't dwell on my situation. Importantly, we often engaged in uplifting conversation. I also used positive affirmations and worked at believing these statements by increasing my enthusiasm for them. Listening to inspirational audiotapes and CDs was integral to reinforcing the general outlook I wanted to foster. I knew these things were essential to leaving the past behind.

When my father passed away some 14 months ago I took a similar approach. We had grown close over the many years we'd worked and lived together up the coast. Just before his funeral, I decided that whenever I thought of him, I would bring to mind the many wonderful times we spent together as lobster fishermen.

In the first couple of weeks after his death I'd recall the pain he suffered during the last 26 hours of his life. Almost immediately I'd feel a great sadness begin to build inside me. But then I would remember my plan to recall our happy times together.

I consistently followed my plan for the next month. After that time, whenever I though of my father, my mind immediately went to all those wonderful times we shared on the ocean. I'd also recall how much we enjoyed our onshore life with the other fishermen. When I did this, a warm feeling of happiness would radiate from inside me. Now it's become habit. I often think of my Dad and it gives me such a wonderful feeling to do so.

I could spend my time telling myself how much I miss him. If I did that, my mind would be immersed in the pain of his loss. This would ultimately be destructive, not only for myself but for those around me.

It's natural that there should be some time to be sad and mourn a loss, but there should also be a clear realisation in one's mind when to end that period and move on. The making of new plans and the taking of action towards those plans is a good way of recovering. When one does this, it opens the awareness and shows us that life really is full of opportunities.

Going through an overly extended period of mourning is destructive to the self. Being aware of our thoughts during this time is one of the most crucial things that we can do. The subconscious in many ways is like a small child—it is very believing. Choosing our thoughts at a time of grief will, to a large extent, govern the length and depth of that grief.

If you establish the habit of choosing your thoughts and become more aware of what you want in your life, you will, over time, begin to leave destructive habits behind. Your tendency will be to think about the prosperous things you intend to have in your life, rather than focusing on what may go wrong. As you do this on a consistent basis those very things will start to materialise in your life.

Often the positive circumstances that come towards you will seem like normal events. But the fact is that when you take action on all of the levels we have spoken about, things begin to happen because of the positive energy you put out. This energy attracts the physical equivalent of your images and goals. Because of this attraction, fortune will tend to come your way. If you are not successful at first, persistence will eventually lead you to success. **It is important to understand that you cannot fail at anything, if you adjust plans and persist.**

After my first marriage ended I feared that things might get worse, and guess what? They did. I had become my own fortune-teller of doom and gloom and, unknowingly, the creator of my circumstances. This was largely due to my attitude, which was based on previous negative experiences. From then on it became my habit to always expect the worst from my former wife. A person with a positive belief system is less affected by the day-to-day trials of life, compared to someone who always fears the next thing that might go wrong.

In 2003 the SARS virus came to global attention. I felt saddened for those who were affected through the loss of loved ones. According to the media hype at the time the virus was going to be as devastating as the great plagues of previous centuries. Interestingly, not as much coverage was given to the advice by world medical authorities that said they had the ability to mobilise counter-measures and stop the disease quickly. In fact, outside China, that's exactly what took place. Authorities also said that the virus was not as contagious as first thought. Yet, because of media speculation and our own lack of consciousness, we, the general public of the world, chose to believe the worst possible prognosis.

In global terms, SARS was far less destructive or contagious than some past flu viruses. But one would have needed to think independently at the time (been conscious) to have had a true perspective on the situation. Terrorism and SARS increased our anxiety to such an extent that some airlines, restaurants and tourist operators were driven out of business.

The lobster industry in Western Australia saw its prices fall dramatically for the first time since the market was established after World War II. Fear stopped people from eating out. This in turn drove the wholesale price of lobster down. Interestingly, previous flu viruses, which killed many more people across the world, never had the same effect on prices.

I believe this was linked to the culture of the information age and the speed with which the fear of SARS spread around the world. We could blame the media and say they need to be more responsible about the type of material they send out. From one perspective this is true. But the best thing, I believe, is to become responsible ourselves for the type of information we choose to consume. If enough people do this, then the media may begin to understand that people aren't buying their message any more. When it hurts their bottom line they will take notice.

The greater percentage of the world's media is only a reflection of the negative thinking that currently dominates in the world. On an energy level the media harmonises with the negativity we allow into our minds and this perpetuates pessimism.

As we choose to change on an individual level, our personal world begins to reflect that change in thinking. This is also true on a global scale. When positive thought expands (consciousness) in a large enough portion of the world's population, then the world's physical reality (including the attitudes of our media) will alter to match that thought energy. But transformation of any sort cannot happen unless it occurs within the individual first. Many people don't understand this very important fact—that the individual has great power.

The more we are dominated by our fears the further we tend to shrink back from life. The anger that is behind terrorism has fear at its foundation. An element of this fear is paranoia which involves aggression to protect and control one's position. This is even though that position may involve killing innocent people. We now have an opportunity to think differently to the way in which we previously thought. Taking a more philanthropic attitude towards developing countries, rather than coming from a superior position, would be a big improvement.

I can't condone terrorism in any form no matter what high ideals are claimed. There is a basic truth to humanity that we are all one (one spiritual entity). When we as a world come to understand what this truly means we will not dare harm another human being. To do harm, is to do harm to everyone. At the environmental level this is much like us polluting the world; if we don't stop doing it, we will eventually poison the planet for ourselves and for all living things.

Our lives are negatively affected when we have thoughts of bitterness, anger and mistrust towards others. As we become more conscious of this, it dawns on us that everything is connected to everything else in myriad ways, and on all levels. This is not something that we have to try to work out intellectually; rather, it is a truth we already know in our hearts.

There was one thing that helped change world opinion and the view of the American public during the Vietnam War, and that was the picture of the young Vietnamese girl running naked down the street, her skin hanging off her body due to napalm bombing. As nations and the world we realised almost as one for the first time (global consciousness) that we were harming children—not the enemy. When at last we see the other as human we will not be able to injure them.

If we wait for the other to take the first step it means we have forgotten one of the most important rules of life and that is for us to **take action if we want things to change**. It's amazing when we take persistent action despite our fear, how that fear begins to shift and then weaken. Even today, although I understand about fear on an intellectual level, I am still a fearful person. This is because those fears are coming from my subconscious.

The subconscious governs our emotional responses to given situations. Of course all of these individual responses combine to make up the personality. The subconscious is the basic operating system that makes the personality function. This is similar to the way Windows is the operating system of a computer. Even though some of my responses are still fearful I now understand that many of these fears have no basis in reality. Knowing this gives me faith that if I confront a fear I will eventually be able to work through it and come out the other side to freedom.

It's been my experience that confronting fear diminishes it. We may not always completely eradicate the things we are afraid of. It's more a matter of those concerns becoming less dominant in our lives. As new affirmations gain a stronger hold in our belief system we will begin living with fewer restrictions. The result is we'll experience an increased level of happiness. At the same time the stress in our lives starts to subside. As a natural flow-on from this we begin to experience improved health.

My situation with ATMs was never fully resolved; the fear never completely went away. There is still the concern of maybe making an error, but concern doesn't evoke the same level of distress as the feeling of fear. If I have a concern with the function of an ATM today I simply ask for assistance from someone at the bank and then logically work through the situation.

I believe most fears can be conquered completely if one desires to do so. Riding a bike was a great fear for me after I hurt my back because it caused me such excruciating pain. The pain would often put me in bed for up to two weeks at a time. My doctor told me that the action of pushing on the pedals and bending forward at the same time caused my damaged disc to protrude into my sciatic nerve. This sounded very logical to me (because it was coming from someone in authority) so I took his advice and avoided the activity. It was only after reading John Sarno's book that I began to think differently.

I had always liked riding bikes, not that I rode very often in my adult life. But the thought of never riding again made me angry. I began to visualise myself riding a black mountain bike. After six months of practising this, my desire to ride grew stronger than my fear of injury.

Our desire has everything to do with our success in conquering fear. Desire is the key thing that drives us towards our goals. But this desire has to be strong. In the case of my bike riding I was very determined. I viewed being able to ride a mountain bike as gaining my freedom from a life spent in bed. As I lay in that bed I would imagine the wind on my face as I rode along. I could feel the warmth of the sun on my body.

When I eventually hired my first bike I quickly overcame any initial back pain. After that I had very little pain to speak of when riding. I was surprised at how I achieved this transition so swiftly and completely. **My visualisation had become reality.**

In other areas like walking, lifting, or sitting I was still struggling. I knew that my desire in these areas was not as strong as it was with bike riding. My only explanation for this is that bike riding evoked a certain level of excitement (the view of the child).

Understanding the true meaning of fear and trust seems simple enough, but applying this to different life situations is another matter. Everything cannot be achieved in a day. Profound changes such as these take time and require patience.

One of the things to remember when tackling fear and learning to develop trust is to focus on one thing at a time. This doesn't mean you ignore the other fears in your life, but it does mean that you should focus on one important goal at a time and build your desire to achieve it. If you do this you will achieve that goal, and more likely at a faster rate than if you tackle too many things at once.

If you're an average human being striving to reach emotional maturity (and that covers the majority of us) then I would urge you to take your time with this process. To become a fully functioning human being is a lifetime's work. Some eastern philosophies would say it takes many lifetimes. I believe there may be some aspect of truth to this view but the full meaning of other lives is beyond my current understanding.

Here is something you might like to consider when you wake up in the mornings to help you gain some appreciation as you go about your journey of life: **This is the start of another brand new day, full of possibilities. Opportunity comes to us in many small and wonderful ways. It may be in the way we greet someone (with a smile), or the way we respond to an inquiry (with enthusiasm). It may come when we approach our everyday tasks from a different point of view, as if they were something brand new, shining and wonderful.**

Taking this approach means that we are applying the law of return. What we give out truly does come back to us and often it is multiplied. Be aware of the energy you're transmitting on all levels.

Make sure it's positive and loving. If you're thinking in a bitter and jealous way you are not likely to experience happiness and joy in your life. A person who doesn't give to other people will find their life is quite empty when it comes to connecting at the deeper levels in relationships. It's important to be generous with your time and to find a kind word for others. People who extend empathy are always happier and they also tend to be well regarded by others.

Fear affects our view in many situations. I remember when I was once at the bank and found myself filling out my withdrawal form right next to two bikies. I felt uncomfortable with these two large men towering over me as I wrote down my personal details. Part of that discomfort came from my past, when I was 18 years of age.

A friend and I had been out on a Saturday night, just strolling around town. We knew there was a popular dance on just down the road, so we decided to take a look. Out the front were five or six bikies. Once we realised this, we decided to give the dance a miss. But for some reason one of the men attacked me. Before I knew it he had punched me in the face and I went down. I decided it would be wise to stay down, and so I rolled myself into a ball and tried to protect my head. He kicked me twice in the body but not with any great enthusiasm. My friend helped me up and we quickly made our escape.

Now you might understand why I felt a little uncomfortable standing next to these men at the bank. Also driving that fear would have been all the bad publicity one hears on the news about bikies.

An hour later after I left the bank I stopped at a shopping centre. When I reached into my back pocket for my wallet, it wasn't there. My mind immediately went back to the bank. I realised I'd left it on the counter after retrieving some details from it that I'd needed. The bikies were still in the bank when I'd left so I knew my wallet would be gone. A sick feeling began to build in my stomach. The thought of losing $250 as well as my credit cards was bad enough, but then I remembered my address was also in the wallet. Images of a home invasion began flashing through my mind. Suddenly my world felt very unsafe.

A little while later, I arrived at the bank in an agitated state and asked about my wallet. To my surprise the female teller informed me it had been handed in. After I signed for it I asked who had been kind enough to return it.

'Two bikies', she said. I was even more surprised to find that all of the cash and the entire contents were still in the wallet. Not a single thing was missing.

For a while I found it hard to believe what had happened—bikies of all people! I could hardly comprehend them giving my wallet back. Suddenly I had feelings of gratitude and respect towards these men and bikies in general. Where had all my distrust and fear of bikies gone? My belief about these men had been well and truly challenged. As with Muslims and all other ethnicities and races there are those who act in a respectful way and there are those who don't.

Remember, the type of action we take is always a measure of the respect we have deep inside for ourselves. In turn, this is a reflection of our fear and trust. We need to challenge our beliefs from time to time and be honest with ourselves about how we formed our views. The fact is that our views could easily be derived from faulty information. This is the only way we can become conscious about the true nature of others and ourselves.

As we continue to question our beliefs and melt away the many facades created by incorrect information, our view of the world will expand. In doing this we are actually rearranging the way our brain thinks. If anyone tells you that this can't be done, don't believe them. Just remember that anything is possible if you apply yourself in the right way.

Over the years I have learnt to reduce and heal different kinds of pain by using my mind in a positive way. The levels of pain we experience are directly related to how we view what is happening to us. It is our level of fear or trust that creates or dissolves this pain.

In healing pain, the idea is to be able—in the midst of it—to sit quietly and remove yourself from the fear associated with that pain. If you can do this you will see the pain alter at some point. Focusing your mind on a tranquil scene is often helpful. Things connected with nature are good, such as visualising a calm ocean or a gentle mountain stream. You might like to imagine yourself in a forest. See it clearly, hear the sounds of the birds, smell the different scents of the plants.

The purpose of this approach is to distract the mind from its normal path of perpetuating fear, because this continues to increase the pain. It is certainly fear that is behind the pain. The problem is many people are not consciously aware that they are suffering from fear. Pain is a natural defence mechanism and it is essential to our survival. The problem is that our mind's view of pain is often exaggerated due to earlier experiences. They could be childhood experiences that do not relate to us as adults today. Yet we may instinctively react from the child's perspective.

I hear some people say that their pain never alters. But the reality is that when we can step back from that statement we will find that our levels do vary considerably. We may experience days or weeks of extreme pain but then inexplicably those levels reduce for an hour or two, sometimes even for a day.

When we are caught up in the cycle of pain we don't tend to recognise these fluctuations, or we discount them. All we recall are the higher levels of pain. This is where fear comes in as it continues to promote the same frightening picture. While this is happening we need to understand that the brain is completely controlling the intensity and the fluctuations we are experiencing.

Books of wisdom have stated throughout the ages: gain control of the mind and you will chart the direction of your life. The same is true for pain; you can gain control over its intensity and in many cases eliminate it. I'm not suggesting that this is easy. But those who choose to take this path will reduce their fear and increase their self-empowerment.

When experiencing high levels of pain, Dr John Sarno suggests that we shouldn't allow ourselves to be frightened by the pain. He also advises taking a strong painkiller and then recommends continuing normal activities. I would also add to this that you must be aware that the painkiller is temporary assistance whilst you work on your beliefs. We are so fortunate that we have the help of modern medicine, especially if it is used in a balanced way. But if you just rely on the medication alone you will not become self-empowered or overcome the situation you're facing.

There are others who are more expert than I in the areas of mind control and pain reduction. But I have personally moved from 15 years of agony to a point where I am excited about life and the future. It's very clear to me that my change in attitude and the application of mind skills have had much to do with the great reduction in my suffering. I expect this trend to continue even though I know there will be bumps along the way. As part of my quest I will continue to resolve fear situations as they arise, knowing that as I do, I will grow mentally, emotionally and spiritually.

7

Overcoming

Overcoming is really what life is all about. Without the intention to overcome we cannot grow. If we don't grow we can't experience the very best life has to offer. But if we dream of winning and think that life will be wonderful all the time, then this is not a realistic view of life. Overcoming means handling the highs as well as overcoming the difficult times.

In sport, a team that consistently wins over a number of years often becomes jaded and complacent. Their victories become harder to achieve on the mental, emotional and physical levels. This is sometimes because their desire is not as strong as it was when they won their first title. They become so used to winning that this success loses its significance. Only after the pain of loss will they come to appreciate the full meaning of winning once again.

Life is consistent with its rules. Understanding these rules will help you even out the highs and lows of living. There is no escape; life is designed this way. Without the intention to overcome life's ups and downs we would just be pushed around by the winds and tides of life. **As human beings we need to chart our own course.**

This book is focused on overcoming illness in the physical, spiritual and emotional sense. It also discusses the basic foundations of financial prosperity. Overcoming the highs of winning is one of the things you will learn to do as you grow. It will help you to keep success in perspective. Once you discover your purpose and work at it, you'll find it will bring you a deeper level of emotional satisfaction. This will result in balance and peace of mind.

The team that wins its first premiership will feel more intense joy than the team that wins several in a row. These first-time premiership winners usually have a far stronger desire. A percentage of this desire emanates from their fan base. Strong desire equates to power, and power equates to energy. This type of power is transferable. When combined with the desire of the team it manifests in the team's physical effort and results in a winning performance.

In Australian football, most experienced commentators will agree that a team playing to a full-capacity home crowd has at least a three-goal advantage. One might ask: if a team has great belief why can't they perform at this level all the time? It is because during 'away' games the opposition team has the advantage of the collective support (energy) of its home fans. **This says something about self-belief—and how fragile it can be.**

Collective desire is a force to be reckoned with. Because of it, it is not unusual to see a team play beyond its generally accepted capabilities, or to win from a seemingly impossible position, even against a team that is superior to them.

Like third-time winners, we also can become too familiar with things. Over time this can lead to our desensitisation. It is much like a beautiful view. The person seeing it for the first time is amazed at the wonderful colours and the striking vista. This feeling creates inspiring energy. But after we've seen the same view on a regular basis it doesn't stimulate us in the same way. This desensitising results in the reduction of positive energy.

I often walk near the river not far from where I live. The scenery is spectacular. I especially like the changing moods of the river that come with different weather conditions. On calm glassy mornings, fish jump into the air, and pelicans trawl for breakfast together like synchronised swimmers. Then there are the windy days with clear blue skies, when the river is filled with the white sails of racing yachts. And, closer to shore, windsurfers with brightly coloured sails sizzle across the surface like silent jet skis.

There is something about large bodies of water that is not only very calming but energy-giving as well. And yet on such beautiful days I see only a few people on the balconies of the luxury homes. Even on weekends they are deserted. Like the football team that is used to winning, perhaps they too have become desensitised.

A reduced appreciation for the beauty of nature in all its diversity can indicate a certain level of despair. Often we may be so busy trying to become 'successful' that we ignore these beautiful gifts. I've also found that a lack of desire to achieve or to embrace life has the same underlying cause. It comes from not being conscious of the gifts we already have in our lives.

Identifying and giving thanks for the good things in one's life not only maintains appreciation for them, but it also increases our energy. This is why individuals or companies that practise appreciation tend to have more success.

If you are depressed on any level, I suggest you might like to consider developing the habit of appreciation. Encouraging appreciation may bring about several changes. Firstly, it takes your mind off what you don't have (remember that what the mind dwells on it also tends to bring into your life) and starts it focusing on the good things you already have. As you concentrate on the positives, depression and apathy are gently lifted away.

When we hone in on the good we find our view of life widens. In turn our energy builds and we are able to take more action on all levels. We may start to find solutions to our problems. It is a simple fact that our physical energy increases in line with the amount of joy we experience.

You may notice that those with high levels of energy are also the achievers in life. This means not only do they gain satisfaction in their work but also in their relationships. It is the area of relationships that will ultimately bring us our deepest joy. When we look back over the history of our life's achievements, it won't be so much the things that touch our heart that we fondly remember; it will be the friends and associates we connected with along the way. **But most of all it will be our relationship with life itself that creates our greatest joy.**

When I first came across this suggestion of appreciation, I wondered how it could possibly help me overcome my constant back pain, let alone improve my financial situation. One of the things suggested in my reading was to start small, for example, by appreciating washing the dishes. Now I thought that this was strange, especially when I knew many people hated doing the dishes. Luckily for me it was a job I'd never really minded doing.

At first I wondered how one could really appreciate doing a job like washing the dishes. It was difficult for me to see any point to it at all. Even so, I was determined to overcome my situation, no matter what it took, as long as it didn't cause any harm along the way.

When I began it was wintertime. As I went about my task I started appreciating my hands being in the warm water. To further develop this habit of appreciation I worked at applying the Buddhist practice of being present. By being present one becomes immersed in the activity they're involved in. This increases the probability of appreciation.

After a couple of sessions I found myself appreciating a salad bowl my former wife had made with her own hands. Then I gained a new sense of worth for the stainless steel pots I cooked in, and the dinner set I used. Even though these belongings were quite modest, my sense of appreciation for them grew. In the end the warm water and the dishes took on a new level of meaning for me. The steps I took were simple but my appreciation for what I already had continued to expand.

Something magical happened from that small act of appreciating doing the dishes—the feeling flowed on to every aspect of my life. I began appreciating the fact that I could stand up (even though I was in constant pain). I was also thankful that I could cook myself delicious meals and was able to appreciate eating them. The fact that I had to lie down to eat most of my meals didn't matter. I appreciated becoming a writer after years of illiteracy. This attitude of appreciation started to affect my whole way of thinking.

The more often I appreciated things, the better I began to feel. Now, my outlook was more optimistic, even though nothing in my life had really changed. This feeling in me started to carry over to the way I treated others. When you feel good about your self you tend to deal with others in a more compassionate way.

For the first time in my life I began to give compliments. In the beginning it felt a bit wooden but after a while it seemed a very natural thing to do. Prior to this I'd already started to compliment myself. I can tell you it took me some time to get used to this process.

If we are not encouraged in the right way when growing up we can tend to be quite critical of ourselves. But if we set about changing our inner critic, the effect on our lives will be profound and positive. This in turn cannot help but flow on to the way we treat others. The end result will be improved relationships.

Recently I had dinner with some friends I hadn't seen for many years. It was an enjoyable evening and I realised how much I had missed them as we talked on through the night. The conversation turned to personal growth. My friend said he remembered when I was fishing that I would put myself down by saying that I'd not been to high school.

He was a well-educated man and had been the head of physics at a leading college for a number of years. Of course he was correct, but back then I wasn't aware that this had become a self-defeating habit, limiting my prosperity. I used my lack of education as an excuse for not being able to achieve my dreams. One thing I'd always wanted was to have a high level of literacy, and also to become successful in business in some way. It's interesting at the time how I ignored my success as a lobster fisherman and skipper.

When we're unconscious about negative habits we are often unaware of how we project these shortcomings and play them out in our lives. We're usually aware of our direct fears about these things but not so conscious when we're using them to create blocks to our prosperity. For example, I wanted to have a high level of literacy because I knew that it would give me freedom in many areas. I rationalised that it would lead to increased knowledge, job opportunities and improved relationships.

When opportunities to be involved in any reading or writing came up I would shrink from them. The very things that were going to give me my freedom I avoided. Why was this? We fear that if we are seen for who we really are, others will reject us. One of people's greatest anxieties is to be rejected by others. I believe this hurts so much because it occurs on the spiritual level. To not be a part of the whole is painful.

This is why we have to push through the pain of embarrassment and be able to leave our fears behind. Each time we do this we grow a little more. With that growth we begin to connect more fully with others. In other words, we feel part of the spiritual whole. Because of this truth, the more often we are able to stretch ourselves, the greater the happiness we will experience.

The truth is many of us reject ourselves first, long before anyone else does. When we are afraid of failing in front of others, because of the fear of rejection, it really is an illusion of our own making. Life teaches us through repeated examples that if we apply the law of persistence, not only will we succeed, but also others will come to admire us for our efforts. People actually grow closer to you when you suspend your fear and face up to whatever obstacle is confronting you.

Admiration is a level of respect, and respect must first come from within us. It cannot be obtained from an outside source. When things are going badly in our relationships we might say to ourselves that he or she has no respect for us. But wisdom would tell us that if we look into our hearts we would find that our thoughts are far from respectful.

Everything must develop internally, not externally. As we come to recognise and appreciate the good qualities we already possess, respect starts to grow within us. When we experience this respect for ourselves it makes us feel good, and therefore, it encourages us to treat others in the same way. By taking this approach we begin to see qualities in others that we had not seen before. Even more interestingly others start to see intrinsic worth in us.

Once we're on the path of healing and we begin to encounter feelings of gratitude, respect, joy and love, we then want to experience more of the same. These feelings do not necessarily materialise overnight. As with anything worthwhile, time and persistence are required. The good thing about this change is that it's not something you have to slog away at day and night. I would describe it more as an interesting adventure, one that continues to unfold over your entire life.

Problems will still arrive in your life (how else could you grow?) but they won't become as stressful as before. This is because you will approach them with a different state of mind (that of love). Instead of worrying about how to avoid problems when they do show up, you will find yourself automatically searching for the solutions.

If we search we will always find. As you gain further experience at overcoming you will start to see the lessons in the problems you've conquered, because there is always a lesson to be learnt. Only when you see this will you understand how it has helped you grow as a person.

As our spiritual outlook develops we don't tend to take life quite so seriously anymore. We remain responsible adults, and yet at the same time we do become more childlike. With this aspect as part of our nature once again we move more easily with the flow of life. Like the child, we see adventure in each opportunity.

We are more likely to move forward in life when we see adventure rather than fear and worry. Taking this approach makes problems easier to deal with. When we see life from this standpoint, the creative mind is freed up to function more readily. By giving ourselves over to our creative side, solutions tend to pop into our head.

I know that with most situations when I'm having trouble solving a problem I just stop thinking about it, knowing that the answer will come to me shortly. Even though I haven't perfected this approach the stress in my life always reduces greatly when I take this attitude.

In my last few years at school I did quite well, but the message my subconscious had adopted was that I wasn't good enough. It's clear to me now that this attitude had much to do with my fear and the way my family approached life.

I never believed or understood that there was anything greater, other than the physical world, where I could go to for help. I accept now that if I had trusted my self and believed in the fact that help would come, things would have flowed more easily for me. When I hand over problems I can't solve to that which is greater, it's amazing where those solutions sometimes come from. And I am not a religious man. All I know is that help is available whenever I seek it.

I remember as a child we used to watch Disney movies that opened with the song *When you wish upon a star*. The lyrics suggested that if we truly believed in our wish, we could make our dreams come true, no matter who we were. How I believed that with all my heart. But by the time I reached my early thirties I'd forgotten the true meaning of those lyrics. Only now do I know the little boy was right to want to believe, because I've since discovered anything *is* possible.

Of course none of those dreams will come true unless you play your part in the grand scheme of things. You cannot 'overcome' without having a dream or a goal to start with. If you place your attention on that dream often and take action towards its fulfilment then this power will assist you in every way. You must make very clear in your mind what you want from life.

It is true that, compared to the animal kingdom, human beings have been given a free will. Unfortunately the majority of people remain unaware about the best use of that will, especially when it comes to being able to get the things they really want from life. When I study people who have been successful in their lives, the pattern is always the same. The first thing they had was a dream, backed by a powerful desire to achieve that dream.

I've found that the most successful people did not initially aspire to having money alone. Many of them had a desire to do something for other people. But don't misunderstand this—they certainly wanted to succeed, but not solely for financial reasons. It could be they wanted to build an affordable car for the common man, like Henry Ford intended. Or it might be a dream like Edison's to bring electric light to every home.

Even though they were dreams of success, they centred on helping others. Financial success came about almost as a by-product of the primary goal. These people knew that a purpose designed to help others would ultimately bring greater rewards.

My studies showed that there were also those who only wanted to help others. Mother Teresa is one of these. She gained enormous joy and gratitude in helping the poor. Her status in the world was very high and she was doing what she loved.

I remember the Australian cricket captain, Steve Waugh, describing in a television interview what it was like to meet Mother Teresa—and how he'd felt a great presence about her. He recalled it as being the most powerful experience he'd ever had in meeting someone.

There is no doubt that over the duration of his captaincy Waugh met many famous people, but what is interesting is that Mother Teresa made the greatest impression on him. I would suggest that because of Mother Teresa's work she developed a powerful spiritual connection with the intelligence that operates the universe. This was most definitely felt by him on an energy level.

It seems that one of the keys to helping ourselves overcome is in the helping of others. This doesn't mean giving help once you're successful. It requires that you do it now, and do so without the expectation of getting something in return.

Sometimes we can find ourselves with resentful thoughts when others don't respond in the way we expect after having helped them. Thoughts of this type can actually block the flow of positive energy. The true act of *giving* means we have to suspend our expectation of receiving something in return.

If you practise giving from this perspective something amazing will eventually happen. It's called 'the law of return'. What you give out will eventually be returned. This works because of the continuous flow of positive energy. For example, if you give compliments you will begin to receive them. But if you think or deliver criticism you will start to receive criticism. After a while this return seems to take on a life of its own (energy flow). No matter what it is (positive or negative) it must eventually manifest itself physically. This can display itself from the way other people begin to treat you, right through to opportunities that increase your income.

Positive thoughts lead to the realisation of dreams. This took me many years to truly understand. It was only when I started to give with a free heart that I began to experience more joy in life. Wisdom tells us that when we give without expecting, we have tamed our ego. If we give and then don't get back what we expect, resentment will build inside us. But if we can withhold that expectation and eventually let it go, wonderful things occur. We begin to receive assistance when we least expect it.

When I first began developing an attitude of service towards others I initially started to help at every opportunity that came my way. It wasn't long before I found my energy was running down. As I considered this I realised I was working too hard at forcing change in this area. I've no doubt that there was a certain level of fear and expectation attached to my approach. After a while I relaxed and only helped when someone asked, and only when I had the time.

One thing I noticed when I stopped expecting anything in return was that I enjoyed helping others much more than at any time in the past. I also realised I had gained many skills during my time running a lobster boat and working with builders. I have added new skills in recent years, in the areas of computing, finance and writing.

When opportunities arose to help others, I noticed several things happening. Firstly, my relationship with the person I was helping always deepened. On another level it improved my self-image. I realised I had a number of very useful skills which I hadn't acknowledged before. Getting to use this range of skills was not only helpful to others but it gave me a lot of joy.

By helping and using these skills I felt myself expanding. When one grows we overcome our fears and experience more of the reality of life. Everyone's life is enhanced in some way—the giver and the receiver.

When I began adult literacy my handwriting was still childlike. I didn't know how to do lower-case printing. I also didn't like my immature signature. After a couple of years studying I expected to improve in these areas. But the quality of my handwriting hardly changed at all. I used to practise by writing affirmations because I knew they would be good mental protein for my self-image. At the time I was going through one ballpoint pen a week, because I wrote so much.

By the end of five years my handwriting, printing and signature were greatly improved. Putting in such an enormous effort to learn how to write was both positive and negative. I was driven by the fear of not being good enough (just like the little boy back in primary school) when I compared my writing to that of others. I'm certain that if I hadn't pushed quite as hard, and trusted myself more, I could have achieved a similar level of writing quality, or better, in a shorter timeframe.

When you are learning something new or trying to improve a skill, make sure you check in with your level of fear or trust. If I'd done so when I was trying to improve my writing, I would've noticed right away that I was feeling fearful. This fear was magnified because I thought I might never be good enough.

If we check in we'll discover straight away whether we are operating from the perspective of fear. Realising this makes it easier to let go of that view. The exercise will often reveal that we are projecting a fearful future. We do this because we are relating a current situation to something that happened in the past. Once we become aware of our behaviour we can then make a conscious decision to return to the present. By applying this skill we discover our fears usually aren't based on reality—only a projected and distorted view of reality.

The first time I began typing on a computer I felt useless. After I learnt to stop thinking about how inadequate I was, I immediately felt better. I also took the attitude that I would continue to improve over my lifetime. In other words, I trusted that improvement was happening even if I didn't have any physical evidence of it. It is a matter of having your goal in place and working towards it in a persistent way, without putting unneeded pressure on yourself. It really is the element of trust that creates this atmosphere.

An interesting thing happened that helped me with my handwriting and typing. It was when I picked up some casual work after many years of illness. This work saw me supervising exams for financial planners and stockbrokers. Once I checked the identities of the students and outlined the exam rules, it left me with time to read or write. I thought I would use this time to work on my book. The interesting thing was that I began to get more of the book written by hand than when I'd been sitting at home in front of my computer.

On the surface, the computer would appear to have a major speed advantage over handwriting. This is true for certain types of work such as the transfer of data. But I found something wonderful happens between the brain and the hand when writing directly on paper—something creative.

The benefits were that I finished my book much sooner than if I had continued on the computer. At the same time my confidence in my handwriting and spelling grew. Over a short period my typing speed improved a further 15 words per minute because I was simply transferring drafts and didn't need to stop to create. My intention was to get the hand drafts transferred as efficiently as I could, and edit and polish later. With this approach I developed a smooth typing rhythm.

When writing by hand I was able to be present and immersed in the story. Transferring the drafts gave me the freedom to type without the concern of creation. Between these two actions my obsession with being a fast typist slowly dissipated. Sometimes we can hold on to things too tightly. When we do this it makes our dreams harder to achieve.

This example simply shows that fear was at the core of the problem. As I let go and allowed the natural processes to take place, my appreciation for my ability to write by hand and to type began to grow. Before, all I could see were reasons why I wasn't good enough at either skill. As I started to see myself as being acceptable in these areas by my own standards, rather than anyone else's, I continued to get even better. My belief once again became reality.

It's interesting to note that before this time, my skills were already in place. The minute I forgot about typing speed, my rate jumped. This example shows how our view of our self can restrict us in any area of our lives. We do this not only where we already have skill but also in areas where we are trying to learn new things.

The example I gave earlier in the book about walking through pain and not being intimidated by that pain is really no different to the typing example. I never considered what I might be able to achieve if I just trusted that what I wanted was possible. My inability to overcome my physical illness was also compounded by the medical fraternity, who unwittingly increased my negative outlook. In their attempts to protect me they told me why I couldn't take part in normal activities. Looking back, I find this approach only served to take away my hope.

I believe part of the medical approach should be about increasing one's confidence in the ability to heal and overcome. Quoting our chances of recovery in percentage terms tends to place us in a box that says we don't have much say in the recovery process.

In the audiotape *There's a Spiritual Solution to Every Problem,* Dr Wayne Dyer relates the story of a woman who was told by her medical specialist that she was dying of cancer. The diagnosis only gave her a few months to live. She chose not to accept treatment or tell any of her family about the prognosis. Then she rented a cabin in the country and spent her time taking long walks in the woods and talking with God. When her stay was over she went home without even visiting a doctor. Nine years after her diagnosis she told Dr Dyer her story.

This story shows us that we have a hand in our own health and that the outcome of that health is connected with what is going on in our mind and in our life. I don't know if I would have the courage to do what the woman in the story did; in fact, I doubt it. But in my own way I have achieved healing in several areas such as chronic anxiety and depression. I have reduced crippling back pain to a level where I can enjoy life with enthusiasm. In time I expect to heal this completely. This attitude alone has to be beneficial to my health. I have completely healed more than 28 years of neck pain, which was supposedly related to a car and motorcycle accident. This was said to be arthritic and deteriorating.

Take all medical advice with due consideration and respect. Whether you decide to proceed with mainstream treatment, something alternative, or make a choice as the woman in Dr Dyer's story did, the determining factor will be your belief in your ability to overcome.

8

Balance

'BALANCE' DOESN'T SEEM like such an important word. Yet putting balance into practice in our lives can be one of the most potent, and yet difficult, things to achieve. For, when we're able to create balance in any situation, the result is clarity.

Seeing clearly requires that several things take place. It means there has to be an alignment of certain facilities. Don't worry; every one of us is born with these gifts. When we see a situation in sharp focus it means we are viewing it with our intellectual mind, our heart and our spirit. At times like this we are able to tap into the higher power of life itself. This is the power that permeates every aspect of life and provides the very energy for its function. It runs the universe in an intelligent and continually evolving way.

Whenever we find ourselves becoming dogmatic about our position over something, we can be sure that balance is missing. If we are trying too hard to solve a problem, the lack of balance tends to put a fog between the solution and us.

Once, when I was studying maths through an external course, I came up against a problem I couldn't solve. The more I racked my brain over it, the more difficult it became. The answer wasn't the problem; I'd already worked that out. It was to do with the system the maths textbook used to arrive at the answer. I just couldn't understand the workings. In frustration I phoned my tutor, but her explanation didn't help me (maths over the phone is not easy).

During all my agitation I knew that I should have stopped work and had a break, but I let my fear (my old nemesis) get in the way of the answer. Trying too hard only increased the fog in front of me. I knew the answer was there somewhere. The other thing I could have done was to move on to some of the other questions, most of which I knew how to answer.

The process of attaining balance begins when we take a step back from a situation. The minute we pause we are able to draw on accumulated knowledge. But more than this, it also builds trust in us that the answer will come. I knew in my heart that on some level I understood the workings out. In the meantime, my tutor suggested sending me some exercise sheets to help.

One might argue that this is just a matter of giving the mind a break so it can produce an answer it already knows. This is partly true, but I'm suggesting that there is another aspect to the equation—relaxing the mind so it becomes more receptive to the intelligent force that is within and around us. This force is part of us and we are part of it.

This process is brought home to me when I set a goal in a certain area and start affirming, as if it's already a reality. When I enhance this affirmation with a visualisation, it's quite amazing how things come into my life to assist me in that area. The interesting thing is that it's quite often outside any knowledge I may have in the field.

I'm not advising that we only affirm and visualise to achieve our dreams. In the case of the maths I didn't read the new exercise sheets, but the solution still came to me the next day as clear as a spring morning. One certainly needs to undertake study in any field they seek to achieve in, but if we work through our heart as well as our mind it will elevate us to higher levels of achievement.

This is the spiritual plane where all answers are available and all things are possible. Men and women throughout history who have achieved great personal goals and advanced the cause of humanity have always stretched themselves beyond the intellectual mind to that which is greater. When we apply trust in this intelligence, not only does it create a calmness of mind but it also makes the mind more receptive to life providing the answers.

In my first year as skipper of my lobster boat I was keen to excel and prove myself. I took a risk with some new lobster pots that I had invented along with three other men. But after a few trials the others quickly lost interest in the pots.

These trials had actually started when I was still working as a crew-member for my father. I convinced him to allow me to trial ten pots. We used to work lines of five pots at the time. With two lines of the new pots it gave me some flexibility to try different areas on the same day.

I kept a detailed record of the lobsters caught from each line. By the end of the season the experimental pots caught 50 per cent more than the traditional pots. This is what convinced me to go with the new pots in my first season as skipper. It was a risky decision. Fishermen are very suspicious of new lobster pots they know little about. The wrong pots can mean the difference between a good and a bad season.

I was so excited prior to the opening day of the season—I couldn't wait to see how well my new pots performed. Unfortunately after the first three weeks it became very clear they were not working.

One day I arranged with a friend to set a line of his pots in between each one of mine. We'd made sure that we both used the very same bait to eliminate any differences. The next day we pulled our gear one behind the other. To my horror he averaged over five lobsters per pot, while my average was only one.

Often when this happens in fishing it can be explained by the inexperience of the new skipper in the way he is setting his gear. But I had 15 years of working the deck behind me as well as intermittent periods when I skippered the boat in my father's absence. I was confident in my ability to set gear, particularly on this piece of ground. My friend had three years of skippering experience and he agreed that the pots were set well enough.

I spent some time considering the situation. My research had shown that the new pots had superior catching ability. During the trials I was the one who set all the pots. Eventually I concluded that there was something the lobsters didn't like about them.

I talked it over with a couple of friends and we worked out what we thought the problem might be. The new pots were constructed out of lengths of black poly-pipe rather than the traditional tea-tree sticks. It seemed, because the pipe was hollow, that it didn't release all of the air trapped in it on its descent to the bottom. This meant that during the night, air bubbles continued to leak out as the pots rocked about with the current.

At the start of the season, the 'white lobster' (so-called because of their milky-pink colour) sit in the sand a metre or so from the edge of rocky underwater ledges. This is because their shells are soft and sponge-like. The 'whites' are always very wary because of their delicate condition. Not only does this leave them vulnerable to predators but it also means they're unable to seek the protection of the rock until they moult and their shells harden up. After they moult they turn a darker red colour and are then called 'reds'.

In the end we concluded that the air bubbles being released throughout the night were enough to scare most of the lobsters away from the pots. This was despite the attractive bait inside.

At this point I realised my mistake. I had conducted my research between the middle and the end of the season. By this time the lobsters had turned red and had moved into the rock, their shells were tougher and a few bubbles didn't put them off. In their hardened state they were now less fearful and more driven by their desire for food and shelter.

Even though the catches of whites were poor for me, the reds turned out to be excellent. The pots' construction—out of the black poly-pipe—helped achieve this result. The black pots blended into the reef and were perfectly camouflaged. I can only conclude the lobsters must have viewed them as part of the reef and therefore a good place to hide. Adding to this attraction was the ample supply of bait.

Despite the poor start I still had a certain amount of faith in my experiment. It was this faith that stopped me from panicking. Faith helped bring balance to the situation. Even though it was only my first season as a skipper, it was balance that helped me view the situation with some clarity.

Experienced people around me were urging me to quickly buy some traditional lobster pots to save my season. I'd seen this type of situation in the past. Panic would eventually overwhelm the skipper and he would rush out and buy the new pots. But rarely did his season improve. One of the problems with new pots is that they take a number of weeks to soak up water and become efficient catchers.

Several things happen when a fisherman panics in this way. His frustration distracts him from concentrating on the job of catching lobsters. When a fisherman's mind is not on thoughts of catching lobsters but rather on what is going wrong, guess what he will attract into his life? That's right—more problems!

It was the balanced approach that led me to have a good reds season. In fact, I even out-performed some of the more experienced fishermen during that part of the season. By the next year I started to use traditional stick pots for the whites and poly pots for the reds. When I worked the reef the poly pots not only fished better, they incurred less damage. A few of the skippers used my pots over the next two years during the reds season and found them to be quite successful.

Fishing was about the only aspect of life in which I had any real belief in myself. Certainly in other areas I was lacking conviction of any type. At that point I had no particular faith in anything greater or spiritual. I would just scoff at the mention of anything like that. My idea of spirituality back then was religion—I didn't know there was anything else on offer.

Faith comes from our subconscious. The subconscious makes no distinction between right and wrong—it simply believes. Once it has accepted information as being the truth, it then makes decisions based on that assumption. This is why we should always examine our beliefs to see if they are based on reality rather than just accept what someone has told us. Remember, the majority of this acceptance would have occurred when we were very young.

About the time my poly pots were being used, timber slat pots were also introduced to our area. The story of the slat pot is an interesting one of belief and imbalance. The slat pot had already been around for some 30 years in the northern part of the Western Australian industry. At the time, records showed that the northern fishermen consistently out-fished the central coast fishermen by a reasonable percentage. The central coast fishermen would justify this by saying that the ground up north was more suited to the slat pot. The truth was the ground was very much the same as where we fished. The lobsters were identical.

Every season or so an inexperienced fisherman would come along and try using slat pots in our area. Inevitably, they were unsuccessful. Once in a while an experienced skipper would try a couple of slat pots but would soon give them away, mumbling about all the things that were wrong with them. This was mostly because their boats weren't rigged up to handle the slat pot. If a boat is not rigged correctly the pots can be cumbersome to handle.

The slat pot is an example of a mass negative belief. As I mentioned before, belief can extend from the individual to nations and eventually become global. Now, and for the past 25 years, the slat pot has been found to be the most efficient means of trapping lobsters known to the industry. Yet for at least three decades before that the central coast of our industry could find nothing but fault with this type of pot. The slat pot is currently so efficient at catching lobster that fishermen would scoff at you if you suggested using anything else.

Here we have something that worked far better than anything else in existence more than half a century ago. Yet the fog of fear, superstition and ignorance hid that truth for more than 30 years, before the central coast fishermen decided the slat pot was okay to use.

Just like the fishermen, distorted views are the very things that hold the majority of us back, and stop us from achieving in life. It's this same distortion that prevents us from seeing the brilliance of our true self. This misrepresentation creates incorrect beliefs that simply do not support us.

Finding balance is vitally important because it is essential in gaining peace of mind. My dear father taught me a lot in this area. He was an emotional man and always approached situations with a level of distrust. I have a mild temperament compared to my father but my belief system was certainly founded on distrust. It wasn't until severe illness came along that I began to view things differently.

I discovered that when I began to trust, things started to flow more easily for me. This doesn't mean that you become naive, in fact, in many ways you become more street-wise. This trust in life will start to provide increasing answers to problems. While this is going on you will also discover that your attitude towards others begins to alter. Where you may have seen reasons to doubt someone in the past you will start to experience an increasing level of trust in them. Even if they do the wrong thing occasionally you will tend to notice this less and focus more on their positive attributes.

Something interesting happens when we begin to trust—situations tend to be resolved in a positive way. At 53 years of age, other than the couple of share portfolios I managed from home, I hadn't been able to do any work due to illness. My financial situation was tough. I owned a few shares but they were down considerably due to the bear market. As well as this I'd lost 40 per cent of my capital in companies that had gone bankrupt. It was clear that the small amount of money I had left in the market wasn't going to save me financially.

I liked the stock market but I realised I had to become better at investing in it. Every day I would affirm that I was a great success in the market and that life was bringing the perfect opportunity for me to increase my income. Six days a week I would do my research to keep up-to-date with the state of the different companies and economies. Just as importantly, I would study and read about successful people in the market to understand what quality investing meant.

One day my sister's financial planner mentioned to her that a private educational firm was looking for people to supervise exams for financial planners. The company preferred people with some teaching experience but said it wasn't essential. On the application I stated my background in share market investing and options trading and mentioned that I wrote a course on options trading which I'd taught to several people. I also told them I was currently writing a book in the personal growth area. The company liked my application and hired me.

It's interesting how things often work out towards one's goals. This gave me some casual work that wasn't too demanding. It also let me rub shoulders with people in the finance industry, which I found interesting. Another great benefit was that it gave me time to write this book. It also left me with enough free hours to research and invest in the stock market.

I was determined to overcome my losses and develop a high quality portfolio, one that had good growth as well as an increasing dividend stream. To achieve this I knew I had to bring balance into my investment approach. Success would also require trust in my growing abilities, trust in the marketplace and giving up my fear of poverty. I knew I would find this last fear difficult to relinquish.

Fear drives one to trade from an emotional perspective, rather than a reasoned perspective. Emotional investing is not based on sound research and experience. This not only creates stress on the investor but also leads to a lack of investment success.

When one has balance in the various areas of life it inevitably leads to success. This is the type of success that does not come from panicky opportunism or from a position of superiority. Balanced success has a relaxed energy that comes from within. It creates an inner trust that life will provide for you. This trust tells you that no matter what, you'll be safe. It also comes from learning from one's mistakes and knowing that you will improve because of those mistakes.

On those occasions when we feel a sense of ecstasy, when we feel a oneness with all that is around us, I would suggest we have experienced balance. **This is because we have let go of our greatest enemy—fear**. The more we incorporate a balanced approach into our lives the easier it will be to overcome fear.

9

Healing

HEALING IS SOMETHING that takes place on an ongoing basis if we are growing. We usually heal in one specific area at a time. This could be in our body, in our relationships, or emotionally or spiritually. Remember that illness in the body is an indication that we need to heal some aspect of the way we live our life.

From the metaphysical point of view, illness is created because of our emotional responses to certain life situations. Eckhart Tolle suggests that the ego is the culprit. He advises that as we learn to dissolve our ego (with all its wrong perceptions of life), pain also dissolves. Sometimes we are conscious of these responses but often they are subconscious and we're not fully aware of what's really going on.

It could be, for example, that we lack skills in communication. Communication is always an internal relationship, in other words, the relationship we have with our self. If we are not supportive and encouraging of our self on our internal screen then we are most likely to be critical of others as well.

Whatever our negative thoughts are (conscious and subconscious) and no matter how much we try to hide them they will eventually be revealed in outward action. This then flows on to adversely affect our relationships.

Wisdom always tells us that *others or life* are not the problem—it is always *our selves* we must work on. I know most people don't want to hear this when they are experiencing problems in life, but it is simply the way it is, and the way it has always been. The sooner we come to terms with this universal law the sooner our healing will begin. Those who choose not to change will experience recurring problems over their lifetime.

Life is about evolution. When we understand this we become conscious and take an active part in our own development. Because of this, life will be continually interesting for us. We will also move more quickly towards our life goals rather than being at the mercy of circumstance.

Life is difficult for some of us and seemingly effortless for others, depending on whether we want to be a passenger or the driver of our life. Some would argue that our development has to do with the evolution of the soul and that our journey is to learn the lesson of love. Still others say that this journey encompasses many lifetimes.

Whether it takes one lifetime or more doesn't really matter. What I do believe is that irrespective of any other lives, the designer of life didn't intend for us to suffer permanently. We have a choice! There is a power that is available to us if we choose to utilise it. I know that if we make use of this power we can turn suffering into joy, and despair into hope. Many successful people throughout history have spoken and written about this power. It is the one thing that is always waiting to assist us in our every endeavour.

I'm not saying I have all the answers—I don't, in fact no-one ever has—but what we can do is apply the collective knowledge and wisdom accumulated from the best of humanity. If we fail to learn from these great teachers then we will remain forever unconscious, and that would be a tragedy. As for many before us, it could result in a life of frustration and suffering.

It's clear that we are advancing scientifically at a faster rate than ever before. Spiritually I believe we are matching this growth.

Between these two areas, our understanding of life is deepening. Our evolution is occurring more quickly with scientific advancements and our growing self-knowledge. Those who don't see this only talk about the bad things they see and hear on the news—I know, I used to be one of them.

If I hadn't consciously decided to change I would still be that invalid lying in bed with debilitating back and neck pain. My mental state would be one of anxiety and depression. Life very likely would have consisted of going to doctors and specialists and living on high doses of painkillers and other medications. It was only when I finally realised that the doctors didn't have the complete solution to my healing and that it had to start with me, that things began to change.

My old neck injury was the area where I'd had the most initial success. Even though I'd suffered from it for more than 28 years, its healing was relatively quick. My pain reduced by 70 per cent over a two-year period. This was mainly achieved through affirmation and meditation. After my first use of Louise Hay's affirmation I went on to create my own affirmations, ones where the words had strong emotional meaning for me.

What we need to do in any area that we wish to change is create positive statements. Use words that have an impact for you. If someone else creates an affirmation but the words don't have significance for you, then the affirmation won't have power to change your situation. Write an affirmation, listen to the words and see if they generate feeling for you. If not, rewrite them until they give you a sense of empowerment as you say them.

Remember, affirmations can be practised out loud as well as in the form of repeated thoughts. I found that writing affirmations down was also very effective. When I say writing, this also includes typing. Whatever system you use, the result is the same—a net boost to your self-esteem. The more you practise this, the more advantage you will get from it.

After you've used an affirmation for some time you may find that it begins to feel a little stale. When this happens, create a new one. The mind loves things that are fresh and new. This also applies to old affirmations you perhaps haven't used for some time—just recycle them. As the brain is reminded of these it helps to drive the original message deeper into the subconscious.

When I create a new affirmation to resolve a situation it can feel unnatural. After I redraft it and work with it a little more, it starts to feel more comfortable. When this begins to happen it means that the subconscious is beginning to accept the message. Using a number of affirmations to resolve the one situation creates ongoing enthusiasm in the mind. Enthusiasm is something we always want to foster because it is essential to overcoming adversity.

The two years of healing my neck didn't consist of constant improvement. Quite often I would slip backwards, and yet I never doubted that I would overcome the injury. After four years I had completely eradicated all neck pain. It has now been a further five years since then and I enjoy driving and other activities as if the neck injury never existed.

Twenty-eight years is a long time to live with chronic pain of any kind. It's difficult for me to convey in words how much this freedom means to me. After years of suffering and unsuccessful treatments I thought neck pain was going to be with me for the rest of my life. This was a condition I was told had become arthritic and would only get worse over time.

Remember, when working at healing any type of illness keep your approach in balance. One can be a self-healer while still accepting medical help. Without a balanced approach there is always the danger of becoming fanatical. I would ask you to keep this in mind because fanaticism can restrict your view rather than open it up.

I've noticed that when I do take painkillers or other medications they can work quite well initially, but with regular use I find the pain often pushes through again. This is because we are dealing with life issues. If we haven't changed the underlying belief (fear) then the brain has the capacity to produce extraordinary levels of pain to overcome any medication.

Dr John Sarno says the brain is creating this pain to divert us from the exact emotional issue that we need to deal with. If, over time, we continue to analyse how we feel about different situations on an emotional level, we will discover things like anger and even rage underlying these feelings. **When these are distilled right down we will find that fear is the root emotion.**

Just realising your true feelings can often bring about the release of pain. Once you set up an affirmation to counteract the fear, you are beginning to play an important role in your healing. If we continue to work on changing a particular belief, one day the illness will start to subside. We have a tremendous ability within us to overcome.

If you take medication I suggest you continue to do so and always work with your doctor. But at the same time you can work with your beliefs and visualisations to mobilise your inner power and advance your healing. If I were to advise someone to quit their medication without anything having been done to change the inner belief that is creating their illness, then there could be serious repercussions for their health. No-one really knows what is in someone's mind—even you. You may understand yourself intellectually but react emotionally in a very different way. So always work with your doctor.

Over time, when you can report success to your doctor, he or she can adjust your medication as required. Don't put pressure on yourself for a quick fix. Just know that you are working on your healing and that it will happen over the right time period for you. Don't judge your healing by my progress or anyone else's. Remember it is a belief that you are working at changing and this is a very individual thing.

I can't say what is and isn't possible to heal but, on a theoretical level, everything in metaphysics is achievable. The key to this will always be governed by what we hold in our minds and in our hearts.

The woman in Dr Wayne Dyer's story who overcame terminal cancer without any medical intervention proves this. She is one of many throughout history who have overcome.

Just as important as working on fear is the need to develop the personality. The two go hand in hand. We can't grow the personality unless we conquer fear. This may mean that at times we experience fear as we stretch our horizons. This is a natural result of trying something new. If we don't stretch ourselves our fear will expand and become our prison.

Another thing we need to do is to appreciate ourselves right now, just the way we are. Learning to appreciate my self has been one of the most difficult battles of my life. Using the Louise Hay recommendation of looking into a mirror and saying, 'I love you', felt incredibly uncomfortable at first. In hindsight it was a valuable exercise, because it showed me that not only did I not value my self, but I also disliked who I was—or, more importantly, who I thought I was. Today I not only like my self but am also proud of who I am and who I've become.

As you work on your fears and heal them one at time, your life will change and improve. In the long term this improvement will be reflected in your body, your relationships and other aspects of your life. The changes I'm talking about don't happen overnight, rather, they tend to appear almost retrospectively. This is simply because we are becoming conscious that change has taken place. If you're consistent in your efforts to improve, change can't help but occur. This is an evolutionary job you've been given. And it's a job that you will enjoy turning up to each day as you progress along your journey.

To heal all of our illnesses quickly would be wonderful but this would also negate one of the purposes for us being here in the first place. I've found that even though I still have some illness, my life has improved immeasurably. There is definitely much more joy in all the daily things I do. I am physically improved in my ability to sit, walk and take part in many things. I still suffer from fear occasionally (as we all do) but I'm not as concerned as I was previously, simply because I know this is a human response.

These days I have a core belief that a solution will be found for every problem. When I'm in the midst of a difficult situation I might still suffer some anxiety, but now there is an underlying belief that I'm truly safe. This is something I'd never felt earlier in my life.

Relationships are now much more interesting for me. If you find you're still suffering from illness but in other areas experiencing increased levels of happiness, or improved relationships, then look to those improvements with gratitude. I suggest you do this for good reason, because it will send a positive message to your subconscious that change is happening—change for the better.

Over the years I developed a fear of catching buses. I'd caught buses up until I was 12 years of age, but when our family got their first car I gradually stopped catching them. At 18 I bought my own car and by my early fifties I hadn't caught another bus. At age 53 my phobia was well-entrenched. Funnily enough, catching trains didn't bother me. Maybe that was because trains tended to run in straight lines and I knew where they were going.

I was unsuccessful when I tried to work through my fear with analysis. In the end I knew what I had to do. First I collected some bus timetables, and then I planned a trip into the city. I sat with this plan for a couple of weeks until I realised I was procrastinating. Within an hour I had walked to the bus station and caught my first bus in almost 40 years.

What an interesting journey that turned out to be. Instead of one of fear it became one of excitement. Suddenly I felt like a child again going on an adventure. Pretty soon I was using pre-paid bus cards instead of fumbling around for change. It wasn't long before I started catching buses and trains all over the place.

Within several weeks of my bus experience I gained the job supervising exams for financial planners. A lot of these exams were in the centre of the city. Traffic was difficult at peak times and parking was expensive. It was clear I needed to take public transport.

The universe is so interesting in the way it works. I decided to heal a fear in a certain area (buses) only to discover I really enjoyed the very thing I feared. Then, once I overcame this fear, an opportunity arose for me to repeatedly reinforce my new belief about buses.

As with any anxiety, the best way to overcome it is to do the very thing one fears. Remember though, approach these challenges gently in small stages whenever possible. With each fear successfully conquered you will gain the confidence to continue moving through other areas of resistance.

As I've said before, you can't put a timeframe on healing because it depends on how deep the individual's fear is. My back injury, for example, has continued for almost 18 years. I have made great inroads in healing it to a certain level but as yet have not cured it. My fear of buses was cured with one bus ride even though this fear had grown and festered for almost 40 years.

You might argue that the back injury is physical and the bus phobia was psychological. This is true, but on a metaphysical level there is no difference. Both illnesses are life illnesses and need to be tackled from either a spiritual, emotional or physical perspective.

Conquering my neck pain was achieved in a way I would never have considered previously. It was healed almost totally through a mental approach (affirmation), which, in turn, influenced my emotional reaction to given life situations. The end result was complete relief from neck and thoracic pain. This was despite being told that x-rays of my neck showed that it had become arthritic, due to previous damage from separate car and motorcycle accidents.

Prior to my use of affirmations, all physical attempts at treating my neck were unsuccessful. In contrast, the bus phobia (anxiety) had resisted 18 months of psychoanalysis and medication. Yet on the surface it appeared that it required a mental solution. My healing was brought about by stopping all mental deliberation about buses, and by simply taking the **physical** action of catching a bus. Many mental strategies are often employed to overcome phobias but sometimes it's better if we stop thinking and just **act**.

Both are examples of the law of action being applied, even though the action taken for both situations was different from what at first appeared necessary.

As I set about healing different aspects of my life there was something that developed in a most natural way, and that was faith. It certainly wasn't something I initially set out to cultivate. It came about entirely as a result of the reduced back and neck pain I experienced. This was simply because I applied a number of suggestions that I'd read about in several books of wisdom. For me it was never a religious faith. If anything I would get annoyed when the word 'God' occasionally appeared in my reading. I remember thinking that I wished the author would just get on with it and give me the information I needed to heal my back or whatever illness I was working on at the time.

The mistake I was making back then was in referring the 'God' word back to my experience with the Catholic Church. As I gained further knowledge I came to realise that this wonderful force encompassed much more than the view of a single religion. After reading and hearing about great leaders from other religions I found that at the core of their beliefs was very much the same thing. This gave me some freedom to reconsider my thoughts on the matter of God.

So the development of my faith was almost accidental, a side effect of working metaphysically at healing illness. I've discovered that my experience is not unique. Many people throughout history have developed faith in similar ways—through the act of overcoming. If you develop faith in your **self**, you will in time increase your faith in life. At this point you may begin to notice a certain flow to the way life functions. Once you arrive at this realisation, your level of trust increases in all areas of your life.

Remember, whatever problem you are facing in your life, it firstly needs to be considered carefully. If a clear answer isn't forthcoming go into meditation. It's a good way of finding solutions to life problems. The answers are often not clear-cut but if you follow the clues they will eventually lead you to a resolution.

If you can't find an answer it doesn't mean that it's not there, it is just the fog that has built up between you and the solution. Often when this is the case it's worth taking action in the best way that you see fit at the time. Even if this turns out to be wrong, it will actually lead you to the right path in the end.

The thing that will restrict your healing more than anything is a lack of action. I used to criticise a friend of mine who is a self-made multimillionaire. When he comes up against a problem he is quick to take action. I, on the other hand, tend to analyse the situation a lot more.

In my criticism of him I would suggest he was like a mouse on a wheel—running madly along but not getting very far. The good thing about my friend is that even though many of the things he tries often fail, eventually he finds a solution.

The best approach is probably a balance between my friend's attitude and mine. I need to think a little less and take more action. My friend would sleep better and have fewer migraines if he stepped off the wheel and didn't launch himself into so many action plans.

Interestingly, both attitudes are driven by a lack of trust in the process of life. My concern is that if I act too quickly I will make a disastrous mistake. My friend's attitude seems to be that if he doesn't act quickly enough opportunity will pass him by. Clearly the truth is somewhere in between.

Happiness is one of the things we all want to experience in life. For Buddhists, this is a key objective. We feel happy when we experience increased levels of joy in our life. When I say 'joy', I don't mean pleasure. To me pleasure is something we seek in order to avoid the pain of life. Pleasure usually doesn't involve growth of the individual or anyone else. Joy, on the other hand, comes by overcoming one's problems (resistance to life) and assisting others to achieve similar outcomes.

When we overcome one of our fears or help someone else in their growth, we will understand the clear difference between joy and pleasure. Joy is something that stays with us and warms our heart, and in doing so it draws us closer to others and the source of life itself. Pleasure is not quite the same. We might chase after it a lot in our life. Sometimes we find it, but then it quickly fades, leaving us unsatisfied and longing for more.

When I was a young man I bought three brand new cars in five years. I would experience great pleasure from the smell of the new upholstery and the quietness of the ride. After about six months that feeling of pleasure would disappear and I would notice little things wrong with the car. When this happened my feeling of pleasure would evaporate. The only thing that would bring it back was another new car.

Joy, on the other hand, has a different texture altogether. One day when I was attending my maths class for mature-age men, one of the students was threatened with being expelled from the course because he wasn't completing any maths assignments. I was certainly no whiz at maths but I was among the top four in our class, so I asked him if I could help.

He looked at me rather surprised. We hadn't associated in class because we had very different outlooks on life. After evaluating me for a few seconds he decided to accept my offer.

'I've never been any good at maths', he said to me as we walked down to the library during our lunch break. 'I just can't do it'. The maths was also new to me but I was managing it okay so I thought I might be of at least some help.

He was a man who had experienced a fairly difficult life. But I could see that his mind was sharp and that he evaluated most things fairly quickly. I also discovered that he'd been a bar manager.

'If I gave you the price of six different drinks could you add them up quickly without a calculator?' I asked him.

'Yes!' he responded without hesitation. That's when I told him he was far better at maths than I was. I told him the only problem he really had was most likely poor teachers in the past.

After 30 minutes of study he began getting the idea and started to solve the exercises quickly. By the end of the lunch break he had finished a fair part of one assignment. I could see the look of joy on his face at having solved the problems he couldn't understand earlier.

'You're the best teacher I've ever had', he said. 'You've got a lot of patience. No-one's ever helped me that way before'.

When I walked out of there I had a deeper understanding of the feeling of joy. Even now, when I think of it, it still warms my heart. Yet, try as I might, when I think of my three new cars I struggle to recapture the feeling of pleasure I once had for them.

The life of Helen Keller is an inspiring example of the idea that, while the world has much suffering in it, the individual can choose to take part in overcoming that suffering. I suggest that all we are overcoming are our learned fears. Once again this comes back to our incorrect views and perceptions of how life works. Of course, the suffering may be a spiritual journey but, as Helen Keller and others have proven, there is also the personal choice of overcoming that suffering.

I believe we have this choice because we have free will. So, whenever life is weighing you down, and you feel that there is not much hope, remember that you truly have the power to change that situation. In the majority of cases, if you change your perception, you will immediately change your feeling for that situation. Once you get to this point you can then start working on the solution.

The one thing I've noticed that often advances our healing is when we give up the need to be right all of the time. This comes from the desire to control our environment. It is not easy for a human being to give up control, because the ego believes we need to be in control to be safe. When we comprehend that we are safe within the process of life, no matter what, it allows us to relinquish control to the natural flow of life. Yes, of course we need to make plans and have goals. After we have created them and begun taking action towards their fulfilment it is then our turn to relax and to trust that life will deliver on these.

The giving up of control, which includes the great urge to make it happen right now, is vital for anyone on the healing path. This was a lesson that took me some time to learn, whether it was healing my body or investing in the stock market. Setting time limits on your goals can be difficult if they are not realistic. So make sure you keep them believable and don't put undue pressure on yourself. Once we come to understand this we start to see the natural flow of life and begin to go with it.

When our resistance to the flow of life reduces, so does our healing begin.

10

Love and Relationships

IT TOOK ME until my fifties to learn about developing trust in an intimate relationship. For many of us this is the area where we have the most to discover about life. In my case the learning period was long and painful. Part of that pain included two unsuccessful marriages. Together these two relationships totalled 23 years of my life.

Looking back I can see that I lacked the skills to get the best out of myself. It's also clear that this lack had an adverse effect on both my relationships. Of course, the same can be said for the majority of relationships that don't succeed or continue in a state of conflict. But if one truly develops their innermost qualities, then relationships will begin to work as a result of that development.

It's interesting how life tends to flow from one thing to another. Often we'll learn something new for a particular reason, only to find it becomes even more valuable in another area at a later time.

This was the case for me after a few years of writing fiction. I felt my skills needed improving, especially from the perspective of my female characters. When I developed female characters I found they lacked authenticity; there didn't seem to be enough depth to their personalities. At that point I decided to enrol in a romance writing course, which I hoped would help me to create more believable characters.

I also had another, more compelling, reason for wanting to understand women at a deeper level. You see, my second wife told me I didn't have a romantic bone in my body. At the time I thought part of what she said was true but I also felt that deep within me there was great romance.

In the end I didn't continue with fiction writing simply because I became so interested in the area of personal growth. But one of the things I learnt from the course was to express my feelings in writing—in particular, my romantic feelings. As far as other feelings are concerned I prefer to talk face-to-face in the appropriate atmosphere. This writing skill was also to become very helpful some 18 months later when I met Zita, the love of my life.

At the root of relationship problems are usually generational issues. Once again this usually comes from our parents or the dominant adults early in our lives. The fact is we all have to learn from somewhere and we are most impressionable when we are young and growing. In my second marriage I became more conscious of this. I would see myself arguing over something that I remembered my parents had quarrelled about.

Even though each relationship for me was different, I started to identify some clear patterns that ran through both my marriages. Of course, if we are unconscious at the time we will most certainly blame the other—it couldn't possibly be *me*! Why won't they change? What I can tell you is that this attitude will keep you stuck for the rest of your life in unsatisfactory relationships.

You might ask how a man with two unsuccessful marriages could be qualified to write about creating happiness in intimate relationships. Firstly I would answer by referring to something Napoleon Hill has expressed in his audio book *Think & Grow Rich*: that failure is only failure when we accept it as being so in our own minds. Since hearing that information over seven years ago I deliberately stopped referring to or thinking about my marriages as failures. I did this for a reason: so that I might learn from my errors.

Marriage is no different from going bankrupt in a business venture. If we learn from our mistakes and keep pursuing our goal, eventually we will succeed. It's likely that we may be unsuccessful more than once before succeeding, but if we make the choice to learn we will without question succeed.

Of course there are those who may think that they didn't fail in their marriage. But this might be for a very different reason. Their rationalisation is one of denial—once again blaming the other. These are often the people who have experienced several unsuccessful relationships by the time they've reached middle age. All their relationships eventually have the same feel, the same flavour. When they take this attitude of blaming the other they have chosen the path of no growth. This only leads to bitterness and resentment and often distrust of the opposite sex.

If one chooses to view things as failure in a relationship breakdown, it can stem from self-esteem issues. This type of thinking can be very destructive if it is allowed to dominate the mind. It was this type of thinking after the break-up of my first marriage that led me deeper into depression, and then to the feeling of hopelessness.

In the joining of two people we must always remember that each partner brings their own set of problems to the relationship. Blame is energy-wasting and tends to attract negativity into our life. So, in my opinion, taking the view of something being *unsuccessful* rather than being a *failure* removes us from the blame game. This is whether we direct that blame at the other or ourselves. It also gives us the opportunity for analysis and to learn from our mistakes.

I agree with Dr Harville Hendrix who contends that dating clubs don't work and that two people should meet naturally when their hearts are drawn to each other. Of course meeting in a natural way won't guarantee a successful outcome if you are both highly emotionally immature to start with.

When you are carrying a lot of baggage from childhood and from unsuccessful relationships you are likely to struggle in your next relationship. For many of us this is difficult to accept when we are on our own and wanting to experience love.

Most of us are aware of women who have been in abusive relationships. When they do meet someone new he often turns out to be of similar character to their previous partner. This is usually clear to their friends but not to them. At the time they are totally deceived by the new romance.

Then there is the case of the nice guy, the one who always seems to get used up financially and emotionally by the women who come into his life. Of course when it all goes wrong he blames her—it couldn't possibly be him.

The fact is, in both instances these people have unwittingly been the architects of their own relationships. This is because what we truly believe and hold deeply in our minds is eventually manifested via thought (energy). The majority of this thought is occurring at the subconscious level. It's subconscious because no-one deliberately sets out to create a destructive relationship. We all want love.

Alexander Graham Bell suggested that the human brain is a sending set and a receiving set to ultimate intelligence. He said, 'What this power is, I cannot say; all I know is that it exists and it becomes available only when a man is in that state of mind in which he knows exactly what he wants and is fully determined not to quit until he finds it'. In this respect, thought (energy) functions like radio waves at different frequencies. Metaphysics tells us that positive thoughts operate at a higher frequency than negative thoughts.

Regardless of how different you are at the beginning of your new relationship your normal behaviour will eventually emerge. This is despite even your best intentions. The same behaviour (thoughts) will most likely result in similar responses from your new partner. And because the responses evoke the very same feelings all over again they frustrate us even more than previously.

Relationships are fated to be repeated unless we make a conscious change in our thinking about ourselves. As we improve our self-image, our view and experience of the world will also become more positive, because we start to operate on the higher thought frequency within the energy field. The energy field is life and everything encompassed by it.

For change to take place you must be relentless in your statements and actions about what you expect to become and have. This is a serious business—there are no half measures. If you don't put yourself wholeheartedly into the process of change then you will be disappointed because change won't happen.

After I had completed several years of personal growth work, I then began to study books and audiotapes on relationships. As I read about some of the different situations that typically arise between couples, I saw how they mirrored some of my own experiences. I liked studying with books and tapes because they gave me the best opportunity to absorb what was being taught. Over time I began to realise why certain things kept occurring in my relationships. With practice I was able to start applying solutions to the different situations that arose.

Once explained, it seemed so clear to me why arguments were never resolved. Of course I'm not saying that I've fully learnt these lessons. But I have experienced how arguments can be diffused, rather than allowed to escalate as they had in my past relationships. Every time I'm able to achieve this, I gain peace of mind.

After the break-up of my second marriage I didn't have an intimate partner with whom to practise, so I decided to apply the theories I'd learnt to the other relationships in my life. I tried out different skills on family members, shop assistants, bank tellers and virtually everyone I spoke to. What I found was that the same basic rules enhanced all relationships. The most important thing was to listen well so that the other person felt understood. (For me, this is an area that is still a work-in-progress and it will probably remain so for the rest of my life.)

When the other feels listened to, their trust in you begins to grow. If you have trust in another you are more willing to open up to them, simply because you feel safe. Once this feeling of safety is established, the lines of communication are enhanced and we begin to experience greater satisfaction in our relationships with others.

I now know that to be a good listener one has to check in occasionally when the other person is speaking. This checking in is to verify that you understand correctly what the other person is trying to convey. It is amazing how often we misunderstand each other. This is because we take one or two words the other person has said and then start applying them to our own view of life. As we do this we actually stop listening to the other person and in the process we miss important information. It's for this reason that checking in is vital.

After we've listened to a certain amount of information, we might say, 'Do I understand that this is what you mean?' You may be surprised by how much of the information you've not heard, or misconstrued. By seeking this clarity we are taken deeper than the everyday surface conversations, which don't give us satisfaction in our close relationships.

The same level of warmth can also be achieved with a complete stranger. The principles are universal. When you connect at these higher levels of communication all parties will experience this as a feeling of positive energy. Each individual will leave the conversation feeling energised and uplifted.

I'm sure we've all had occasions when the person we were talking to was not listening to us very carefully—or, worse still, only paying us lip-service. We pick up on this instantly. When we see the other person's eyes stray a little we know they have stopped listening and are thinking about what they are going to say to us. Once this occurs the golden rule of communication has been broken: **first and foremost to make sure the other person feels understood.**

A safe environment can't be created when we feel we are not being listened to. This tendency to not listen is very common. Even if we are working at becoming better listeners, it still happens. So the practice of checking in with the speaker occasionally brings us back into the conversation and keeps us informed as to the speaker's true meaning. When we do this we actually become more interested in what the person has to convey, and they in turn will truly feel listened to. Then the lines of communication have been strengthened.

One thing to remember is, don't check in too often. You must allow the other person to convey what they're trying to say. Constant interruption will stifle energy flow and create frustration on the part of the speaker.

The minute we sense someone else understands us we immediately warm towards him or her, because as we feel listened to we also feel cared for. Inside us all there is a yearning to be taken care of. There is nothing wrong with this, as long as it is not a dominant feature of our personality. Otherwise we become too dependent in relationships.

Another important thing I've discovered is to ask the other person how they feel about a given situation. If you ask them what they think you will often get a more superficial answer. When you understand someone's feelings about something you are then able to empathise with their concerns.

It's this act that moves the relationship to a higher level. If this is applied in an intimate relationship, along with love and a sprinkling of romance, it can lead to the most exquisite life-long commitment to each other. It will become not only a relationship that both parties enjoy but one that they deeply *desire* to remain in. This is very different from staying because you need to or have to.

It's much like a wonderful adventure that keeps revealing new treasures about each other. This experience will create joy and excitement, not only towards each other but also in the things you do. Your confidence will grow knowing that you have the skills to create this atmosphere.

Those who say that a couple cannot live a lifetime together and continue to feel the same depth of love for each other have not looked around and seen the people who have achieved exactly that. I believe this type of relationship is only possible when both people are actively involved in growing personally, emotionally and spiritually.

If one party is growing and the other is stagnating then the relationship cannot remain in a state of happiness for very long. The other thing that must happen is for each person to make their partner and the relationship a priority. This priority comes from a sense of giving out of love rather than out of obligation. When this is practised one will experience a deep sense of love within the relationship.

For a relationship to be truly successful, partners must make their feelings known to one another. But this has to be done in the right way. Many times in my own marriages, if I didn't like something my wife was doing, I would complain about it in an accusing way. This is a common problem in relationships. Unfortunately, when it becomes a habit it destroys mutual respect and trust.

Rather than bring you the things you want, criticism will simply create more tension between you and your partner. I believe the majority of people understand this is causing damage even when they are in the act of criticising their mate. Unfortunately most don't know how to stop it from occurring. Some continue along this line for years, often going to their graves blaming the other for various injustices.

The question to ask yourself is this: do I want to continue experiencing conflict or do I want something better for my relationship? The solution in many ways is simple: tell your partner how you feel. You do this in a specific way. Never, never approach them in an accusing or threatening manner. I remember the first time I experienced conflict with Zita I immediately shrank back and went quiet. As a child I had reacted that way when my father lost his temper or if there was any conflict between adults.

For some reason with Zita there was a tone in her voice that left me feeling like that little boy in Year Three—the one who was made to stand in front of the class and was told he'd not only failed but also had let the whole class down. With considerable apprehension I decided to try some of my newly learnt communication skills.

'I feel like a scolded little boy when you're sharp with me', I said. 'It's as if I've done something wrong to hurt you and I don't know how to fix it'. This was very hard for me to say to Zita because I cared so much for her and didn't want to upset her in any way, or threaten our relationship. She was also aware of my Year Three experience. Remember, this was my first shot at using my new skills in an intimate relationship, so I was pretty nervous.

To my surprise the whole atmosphere changed. Zita's attitude softened immediately and she told me she wasn't even aiming her anger at me. The problem was a number of things had built up during her day and a situation that occurred in the kitchen was the last straw. I just happened to walk into the middle of that frustration. We then gave each other a gentle hug and both felt better, not only because we understood how each other was feeling but also because we expressed empathy towards each other.

That new approach helped set the tone of being able to truly express our feelings to one another. In the old days my initial reaction would have been one of the frightened little boy—but only for a short while. Not long after, my resentment would build up. I'd probably start using accusing words such as, 'What right do you have to speak to me that way?' Or even worse, because the relationship was in its infancy, I might easily have said nothing all.

The problem with this last approach is that it internalises anger. If the situation is repeated, hostility increases because of this accumulated resentment.

Telling someone off for expressing their anger immediately makes them wrong. If a person is told they are wrong they almost automatically feel attacked. This is exactly the opposite of what one wants to feel in an intimate relationship. Expressing anger is an important thing, although it is vital to do it in such a way that doesn't threaten others. Instead of exploding and attacking the other person it is more helpful to say, 'I feel very angry when you don't help me. And it leaves me feeling unappreciated, as if I have to carry the whole load. What I want most of all is for us to be a team and to support each other'.

When you express your anger in this way your partner is truly able to hear your concerns. Your partner may have no idea you felt this way. In a committed relationship we often assume our partner knows what we are thinking. In many areas we also believe we can sense what they are feeling or thinking. Sometimes we are correct in our assumptions but just as often we can be off the mark.

When we've been in a steady relationship for a while it's easy to start believing we have a crystal ball connection to our partner's mind. But mind-reading will never deepen the quality of your love as much as applying communication skills and expressing your feelings to your partner.

Over time I've learnt not to take anger so personally. I've also become better at reading the landscape. In other words, if I notice a change in Zita's mood, I'll ask how she's feeling in general, or about something in particular. This way, if there is anything bothering her it gives her the opportunity to talk about it. Zita is particularly good at doing this with me and with others. I've learnt a lot from her about being perceptive in a relationship.

After a while we learn to tell our partner how we're feeling. This creates a natural habit fostered in an atmosphere of trust and love. But this doesn't mean one stops asking one's partner how they feel, because to ask is an ongoing act of love. It's also a good thing to practise at the end of the working day—but don't forget to apply the check-in rule.

Of course one doesn't ask the other person how they are feeling if it's clear they want some quiet time on their own. Given space you will find they will be quite happy to talk later on. By taking this approach we have both found that we feel calmer within ourselves and in our relationship.

If someone is under pressure and there is an opportunity to help—go ahead and do so. Even if the other person's temper is rising, just go about your task in a quiet, supportive fashion. Initially it may seem as though your efforts are not appreciated. This is the point where you need to remove your ego from the situation. In time you will find your assistance will be acknowledged if you don't seek the pat on the back. As you help, the other person will feel comforted and this in turn will cause them to develop an appreciation for you.

When one feels supported in an intimate relationship or any other, there are fewer and fewer reasons for frustration. I must clarify this by saying that you don't give this support to someone who is a bully and who has no intention of changing. The people you allow into your life must have a willingness to improve themselves, and to also support you in pursuing your dreams.

When I met Zita, I began to feel truly supported for the first time in a relationship with a woman. Not only was I given praise for skills I possessed and used, but more importantly, I was appreciated for who I was. At every turn I was encouraged. When you feel loved in this way it only makes you want to return the gift. You start to give without expecting because it becomes your natural way of being. In fact, at your core, it is your natural way of being.

Some of these communication skills may seem basic, yet not many of us practise them in our significant relationships. It's so easy for bad habits to continue from our childhood or from previous associations. Good habits are skills—if we haven't been taught them, how would we know what they are, or how to apply them in our lives?

I would encourage you to invest in books or CDs in the area of relationships. You don't have to become an expert for your relationships to improve dramatically. By just applying a basic understanding of the laws of good communication you'll be amazed at the positive effect it has in your life.

To create a successful relationship you need to work on yourself. This includes reducing your fears and developing a deep trust in life. Finding your life's purpose is crucial here, because working at your purpose will fill you with joy and make you more interesting to be with. It's only when you've spent some time working at these things that you will be better prepared for an intimate relationship.

Unless you develop in these different areas you may well enter a new relationship with wounds that are just too much for the relationship to carry. If we begin an intimate relationship severely wounded it means we are not going in with our best chance. It also says that we are being unfair to our new partner. It truly is up to us to take the initial steps and do the work required to heal the damage from our past and to evolve as a person.

Resistance to this suggestion comes from the child within who wants to remain safe and protected from the big bad world. The wounded child's view is: if there is no change then there's nothing to fear. I'm not suggesting that you have to solve all of your problems. But if you heal some of your outstanding issues, not only will you feel much more comfortable with your self, but you will also experience greater happiness in your new relationships.

If you are single and living alone, once you begin healing the different problem areas of your life, living alone will cease to be a big issue. That's because joy will start to develop in your day-to-day living.

You are not here solely to improve yourself, or just to attract a partner (although attracting a partner might very well occur as you evolve personally). Your role in the great scheme of things is far more important than that. I believe it is to discover your purpose and to live your life from a conscious and compassionate perspective. By developing this purpose you are able to fulfil the plan that life has for you. An individual's purpose is part of the overall plan of the universe. The intelligence that is life wants us and the universe to evolve.

If you follow your purpose and truly put your heart into it, the things you desire may very well come into your life.

Once I had completed several years of personal growth work and made some progress in my physical condition, I decided it was time to get involved in a relationship. When I say 'decided', it was more a feeling than a clear decision. It came shortly after I'd bought my mountain bike and had been riding it successfully for a while without back pain. I'd practised the visualisation of bike riding so often that it felt real to me. Because of this positive result, I thought why not create a visualisation for a relationship?

One night I sat down and wrote a list of the things I sought in a woman. I was fairly specific but at the same time didn't go overboard. A loving, supportive woman was essential, as was one who accepted my love without rejection. It was important for me not to have a partner who withheld love or rejected my love as a means of control. I also wanted to be with someone who had an interest in other cultures and who didn't suffer from racial prejudice.

Now that I was older I understood that I also needed someone who could hold a good conversation and who was reasonably articulate. Two major requirements were that she supported my practice and study of metaphysics as well as my spiritual outlook. My physical desire was for a tall woman, five foot ten inches, of slim build, with short black hair. Don't ask me why (I'm five foot seven inches), I just liked the idea. One of the other fundamentals was having healthy eating habits and flexibility with different foods.

I wanted a woman with good moral values and one with a belief in God. This last stipulation was interesting for me because it was something I'd never considered in earlier years. There were other details, but these were the fundamentals.

I remember telling a friend one day that I was going to visualise a girlfriend who was five foot ten with short black hair and a slim build.

'Why do you want someone so tall?' he said, completely ignoring my concept of visualisation. From that point on I never again mentioned the process to him. But for ten minutes, twice a day, and for more than a year, I continued with the visualisation. By the end of that time I started to think I might be wasting my time. Suddenly, one day, a woman fitting the description came into my life. Within two weeks another appeared. While I was evaluating this, an opportunity came up for me to go out to my first dinner in two years. Even though I still had some trouble sitting down I knew I could manage it with painkillers.

The dinner was at a local Croatian club. We sat at a long table, set for around 20 people. There were 12 in our group, of whom I knew about eight. Not long after, the others arrived. Among them was a tall woman of slim build with short black hair. She resembled my visualisation more closely than either of the two other women.

As the dinner progressed I couldn't help but look up and wonder about this interesting woman—after all, I felt I had known her for almost a year from my visualisations. By the time we'd finished dessert I had an overwhelming urge to meet her. The only problem was that I was a shy man and had never really put myself forward where women were concerned. If they came my way that was fine, but I'd never tried too hard. This time things were different. I felt a strong urge to meet her. It wasn't anything like my past where there may have been a powerful sexual attraction, although that was certainly part of it. This was more like a wonderful mystery I needed to solve.

Almost before I realised it I had picked up my chair and gone to the other end of the table where she was. There were two people seated there who I knew and they introduced me to everyone. Someone asked me how I liked the Croatian food.

'It was great', I answered. 'It's just like the food my neighbour used to cook when I was a boy'.

'What was her name?' Zita asked. When I told her, it became apparent that my old neighbour was also a friend of Zita's mother. So that night we had a short but intriguing conversation, as much as one can have when there are 70 other people in a very noisy dining room.

My interest had been aroused so I was keen to go back to the Croatian club and hopefully talk to Zita again. From the second meeting our regard for one another continued to grow. Not only was there a wonderful mutual attraction but also our conversations differed from those I'd had with other women. There was an honesty in our communication which I'd not experienced before.

Another thing I liked was the dignity with which Zita conducted herself. From the start it was clear that she had high moral values and worked at applying them in her life. We found we matched up in many ways. There were differences but these were not extreme and so therefore they were interesting.

As our relationship progressed I was stunned by some of the conversations we had. This was because those conversations matched almost exactly the visualisations I had created. I would imagine the words we would speak and the way we might hold each other. Our dialogue was always loving, supportive and encouraging of one another—and in reality that was the way it turned out.

One of the earlier authors I came across who explored visualisations was Brian Tracy. When I listened to *The Psychology of Achievement*, I simply believed that what he said was true, because it sounded sincere. As I've mentioned earlier I didn't find it easy at first to create visualisations, but with dogged determination I applied the information I learned from his audio series. I'm surprised by the areas where I've managed to make visualisation come true in my life.

Because of these experiences I developed the firm belief that life works on an energy level and that your imagination is a major force in creating your life. Your reality is a result of the dominating thoughts you hold in your mind—the ones you believe at the deepest level. Even today I don't spend the time I probably should on visualising what I want in my life. It's one of the areas I hope to improve in.

I truly believe in visualisation because I've experienced its power at work in my life in overcoming illness, in becoming a writer, and in attracting a loving partner. I look forward to my ongoing adventure in this area.

When you consider the people in your life, be honest with yourself. What do you really think about them on a regular basis? I'm sure you'll find the reality of your relationships match perfectly your innermost thoughts. So if you truly want to change the quality of any relationship you first need to change the way you think about that person. The choice is always yours—first comes the thought, then the reality. It's the way the system has always worked. You must choose a positive, loving view if you want that type of relationship with your self, with life and with others.

11

Manifesting

To 'manifest' something metaphysical on the physical plane requires the consistent application of thought. By applying your mind in a deliberate way you can manifest the things you want in your life. The old saying that says it takes hard work if you want to get anywhere in life is paradoxically false and yet true at the same time.

The great achievers throughout history have used methods other than hard work alone to make their dreams a reality. Marcus Aurelius said, 'A man's life is what his thoughts make of it. Our life is what our thoughts make it'. As I've mentioned before, this kind of achievement is different from the drive that is born out of fear. I understand only too well the anxiety behind this type of application. The people who really excel have balance in their lives—they believe in the power of their imagination, they work hard, but they also have fun along the way.

When I was fishing in my later years and earning good money, I found that the business was only exciting when I caught a large number of lobsters. That feeling would soon disappear when the catch fell. In fact, I hated going to work most days. This contrasted noticeably with my first nine years in the industry. Back then I used to wake up with a feeling of excitement about spending a new day on the water.

The difference in my emotions came about because of intention and balance. In the beginning I was fishing for the love of being on the ocean and to experience the life of a lobster fisherman, and all that that meant. During that time I was overjoyed just to be out on the water. At dawn I'd be leaning over the side of the boat to get a glimpse of what was in the first pot. I could hardly wait to see what we'd caught. To watch the sun rise over the land, and to catch the scent of the Australian bush that drifted to me on the light easterly wind was wonderful.

I still remember my feelings of delight over the blueness of the ocean on a clear summer's day and the kaleidoscope of colours provided by the different species of fish. I loved the mystery of the waves on the outer reef and the brilliant white sands of the beach. Certainly, I wanted to be a success financially but it was the overall life that I loved.

Complementing my time on the water was my onshore life. We lived in a camp in the small fishing town of Ledge Point. Our camp consisted of five huts in which a dozen or so fishermen lived. Most of these men were southern Italians. There were approximately 100 people living in the entire town at the time. A reasonable percentage of these were of European extraction. I found that the mix of nationalities made life interesting.

In those days, Ledge Point was also a low-cost holiday spot off the beaten track for a number of city people, especially those who liked to relax near the ocean. During holiday times the population would often double. I used to look forward very much to the holiday season. Throughout my teenage years I made some good friends among these city holidaymakers.

I mention these things to give you a picture of the life I enjoyed at that time. Unbeknown to me I was using the skills of metaphysics to create that life. Yes, there were also a number of not-so-good things that happened over that period, like seeing our boat wrecked in a storm, and having my heart broken by a beautiful young girl. Occasionally I'd have to put up with the ugly face of racism. Yet I never seemed to be disheartened for very long by such events. I know it was because my mind was immersed in the beauty of the ocean and all that it did for me, as well as the promise of a wonderful future ahead.

When I say that I was using the skills of metaphysics to create my life, I mean that my mind was filled with all the good things I **thought** would happen. If we understand and accept that the universe operates on an energy level and that thought manifests on the physical plane, then it follows that this is why I had so much enjoyment at that time. For example, when our boat broke up in little pieces on the shore, I was excited. I remember my father asking me what I had to be happy about. I quickly replied, 'Now we can build a new boat with the insurance money'.

At the time it didn't matter to me that the insurance cheque wouldn't be enough to cover the cost of a new boat, or that Dad had a partner who wouldn't be interested in rebuilding. I'd been having dreams about us owning a new boat for some time. I just assumed—and believed—it would happen.

So my early years fishing were a time of enthusiasm; a time when I believed deeply that wonderful things would happen. And that was very much the reality I experienced. It didn't concern me what problem came along, I just knew we could overcome it.

This was certainly in stark contrast to my later years of fishing. It seemed I was obsessed with surviving in the world. By the time I was 27 I started to feel the weight of responsibility. My thoughts of enthusiasm were still there but they were beginning to be overshadowed by concerns of what might go wrong. I'd still go about solving situations when they arose, but even so, the adventure of life was becoming harder to find.

This deterioration seemed to occur without me being fully aware of it. When one is young and has not encountered much stress in life it's easy to be resilient for a while in the face of adversity. Pressure only starts to become a problem when we're not aware that the fearful thoughts we harbour are actually creating that stress. When this is the case and those thoughts are allowed to continue unabated, they will expand, and at some point manifest in our lives.

My increase in fearful thinking began when I experienced several months of breakdowns with a new boat I had built. After that, I felt the pressure mount. Even when things were going well I'd hardly acknowledge them because I was waiting for the next thing to go wrong. Sooner or later this expectation would be fulfilled. **Whatever the mind dwells on it will eventually bring into reality.**

Feeling responsibility the way I did soon exposed my low self-esteem. This had never surfaced in my early years fishing because my father was first in line to take the strain. The interesting thing was that in my father's last few years I largely took charge of preparing the boat for the new season. I also solved the day-to-day operational problems during the season. But at the emotional level I still didn't feel ready for responsibility.

The fact is, psychologically, I would never have been ready because poor self-esteem was the underlying issue. When this is the case, it is difficult to feel in control of one's life. People suffering from a poor self-image can still be successful in given areas but they will struggle to create overall balance. For example, a person may be very successful financially but have poor-quality relationships. This of course can cause family problems or a lack of satisfaction in other relationships, because of the inability to communicate well.

When a life is out of balance over a period of time I believe illness is created in the body. Serious illness can be manifested quickly. This will depend on the depth of emotion held within a belief system. Louise Hay's explanation of cancer and how it may often be related to long-held bitterness has always made sense to me.

Recently, I heard of a man who died of cancer and then, six months later, his wife died from the same disease. It's possible the wife felt such bitterness towards life for having taken her husband away that unconsciously she manifested the disease over that short period.

On the healing side, I believe this is no different from terminal cancer sufferers who overcome their prognoses. We often hear that those who've beaten their disease have made major changes in their lives. By creating these changes they bring their lives back into balance and manifest their good health. In the act of overcoming they may very well have let go of some deeply-held bitterness and embraced life more fully.

The opposite may be true for the person whose illness is worsening. By holding on strongly to hatred, bitterness, or rigid views, they may be restricting their ability to embrace life and therefore the possibility of healing.

It would be unfair to say that those who aren't healing don't want to. We must remember that we are dealing with a lifetime of emotional–environmental factors that have created our outlook on life. I'm simply hoping you will consider what I'm suggesting. There is no blame here. Thinking about this at a deep level may assist you in changing your situation and help you to overcome your illness.

I'm sure that many doctors would agree that one of the major hurdles they face in treating serious illness is the attitude of the patient. Depression reduces the effectiveness and outcome of any treatment. In the end, it's your personal decision, but I believe you are not limited by an illness. When you understand this, you can be either the continuing creator, or the healer of that illness.

I believe we are in a constant state of manifesting. We should be aware that our thoughts are the first steps towards creating the very life we experience. Few of us were brought up in the perfect environment, and for this reason we are very likely to have some distorted views of life. It's this distortion that stops us creating the life we really want. The more we let go of our limiting views, the more we will realise that life is a creative adventure.

When I met Zita at the Croatian club, friends and family had been trying to get us together for a while. But what those people weren't aware of was the specific visualisations I'd been working on for 12 months prior to that time. On an energy level they had become part of the frequency that drew Zita into my life. The fact that later a number of our conversations and interactions matched my visualisations so accurately was no accident.

I must point out that these opportunities wouldn't have arrived for me if I hadn't simultaneously been working at improving my relationship skills—most importantly, my relationship with my self.

Things such as positive affirmations and visualisations, combined with action towards your goals, will always help you create the things you want in your life. When the opposite is true, guess what you will be manifesting? That's right—all your dominant fears.

Your level of success, happiness or health can be traced back to your deepest beliefs. This is why it is so important to begin to learn to use your mind in an intelligent way. One of the most wonderful things that could occur on this planet would be for human beings to use their minds to benefit themselves and their fellow humans spiritually.

I hope that by now you are getting a sense that everything is truly connected on all levels in the energy field—'God' or 'life'—call it any name you are comfortable with. Every thought we have is action in motion and it has a definite effect on us and everything around us. Be under no illusion here: you can't manifest success in any area of life if your mind is preoccupied with your fears. Our most profound discovery in life will be when we come to understand that this force truly exists. And not only that, but that it operates every moment of every day, whether we believe in it or not.

It is still my belief that going to war has never been the way to resolve problems between countries; neither does it create lasting peace. The Cold War was a result of fears held in the minds of nations about the other. The massive arms build-up that led us close to a nuclear disaster was simply an accumulation of those fears. Currently, east and west have reached a similar stage since the September 11 attack on the World Trade Center. This is the breaking point where each side stops seeing the other as human.

Once again we cannot solve conflict successfully by totally laying the blame on those who oppose us. Both sides need to take a different kind of action if the world is to reach the place of peace that all of us desire deep in our hearts. As always we do this by inconspicuous means—by using our minds at the spiritual level. This requires us to place ourselves in the other person's (or country's) position and view their situation with compassion. When we begin to practise compassion—truly practise it—we once again start to see our opponent's human qualities. As we reach this point the probability of a solution arises.

One thing that moves us forward more quickly in conflict-resolution is having the ability to step aside from what we see as our just and rightful position. Insisting that we are right and the other is wrong means we are coming from a position of superiority.

When we look more closely at superior attitudes we find they tend to emanate from a foundation of fear. We fear being wrong (the fear of making a mistake) and we fear we'll be hurt in some way. Some people with superior attitudes can also be aggressive. This is an attempt to protect themselves because of their own perceived fears.

Having entrenched views means we have narrowed our outlook. And a reduced outlook lessens the chances of resolving any situation. This need to be right can be expressed for a number of reasons, ranging from the personal, to family concerns, or, in the case of countries, for economic, political or religious reasons. When these concerns are distilled right down, it is always revealed that fear is at the core. In the end, if we use our minds in a compassionate way towards the other, we will transcend our own fears and truly open up understanding between each other.

Understanding is a fundamental element of trust. When trust is built at the human level, entrenched views tend to dissolve. As the Berlin Wall came down, people in the western world began to view East Germans as human for the first time in a long while. The only thing that had changed was a point of view.

The type of government a country has reflects the fearful or positive thoughts of the people it represents. If we continue to grow personally as well as spiritually, that growth will be reflected in better quality people at all levels of government. When this momentum builds globally we are more likely to manifest world peace than we are whilst dealing from a position of fear or superiority.

This view of manifesting has been pointed out to us across the history of human kind. The Buddha said, 'All that we are is the result of what we have thought. The mind is everything. What we think we become'. Jesus said, 'Even the least among you can do all that I have done, and greater things'. Albert Einstein implied that logic will take you from one point to another—but imagination will take you where you dream of going.

In the developed world this approach is now also supported by some in the field of psychology. The central belief is that the content of an individual's mind or the collective psyche of a group is the causation of their reality. So, as we gain true control of our minds, conflict will diminish and solutions will appear.

I believe that the individual and global resolution of conflict cannot be achieved purely through an intellectual approach. It must include the deliberate act of compassion in all minds. Whenever you approach any matter with compassion it begins to lift you into the spiritual realm. This is only natural because when we strip away our fears we are left with who we truly are—spiritual beings.

I can't claim to be an expert in the area of manifestation. At this point I haven't made my fortune—but I expect to do so. Expectation is an essential ingredient in the pursuit of any endeavour, it fuels our desire to reach our goals and fulfil our dreams.

Opportunities are beginning to come to me now, opportunities that I've never encountered before. Even if they were presented to me in the past I would not have recognised them as such. Now I see these possibilities because my self-image has improved. To me these opportunities are a clear example of the field of energy in operation.

Twelve years ago I decided to learn about derivatives and the stock market, in order to educate myself in an area that had always been a mystery to me. Because of my enthusiasm there was a natural flow of connective energy. Henry Ford likened enthusiasm to yeast in bread. It raises your hopes and further fuels your desire, thereby increasing **energy** to reach your goals.

My new learning led me to manage someone's share portfolio a couple of years later. It was a rocky road, but I learnt from my mistakes by letting go of all the hype which often surrounds investing.

During this time I began to understand and assimilate the principles of long-term investing. I learnt how to analyse stocks by reading the books of successful investors. Each time I read another book there was always something new I would learn.

Meditation was effective in the area of investing because it helped me to see through the conflicting advice of many analysts and the panic that often pervades the market. Over time I've found that meditation has given me clarity in my decision-making. I often 'feel' my trades at an energy level. The feeling is much like I've described in my walking exercise in Chapter 2. Relying on this works very well for me, but I only ever take action on this feeling after I've first completed my research.

You must always take physical action in the world, as well as the action of following your inner voice; remember, the two things are interlinked as co-creators of your life. Affirming the outcome you want by way of visualisations and positive statements is also an important part of that creation.

I didn't have a personal mentor but I did find a newsletter that was regarded as one of the most reputable in the country and had investors' best interests at heart. This helped to develop my core understanding of long-term investing. Investment newsletters that are full of flashy advertisements mean that the publishers don't have to work too hard for their money, because their income is secured from the advertisers. I also think it leaves them open to a certain amount of corruption. Advice from these sources needs to be viewed with caution.

If you're enthusiastic and consistent in your approach about growing and educating yourself, the intelligence of life will always come along to assist you. Whether or not you believe in a universal power, believing in and working towards your goal is sound practice in becoming successful at whatever you do. I don't know of any great achievers who did not spend time and energy educating themselves in their field. And their chances of reaching their dream would have been zero if their dominating thoughts were of failure.

Occasionally, I see interviews on current affairs programs with people who are unable to get a job, despite numerous applications. When a life coach is brought in to assist the person, it becomes apparent in most cases that the core issue is a lack of self-esteem. After a few weeks or months of working with the coach, the person usually finds a job they like. It may not necessarily be their dream job but it gives them the beginning they need.

The reason many of us do not succeed is because of the self-image movie that is playing in our heads. Change the movie (by reshaping the self-image) and we begin to get a different response from the world.

The initial interview with the life coach will usually reveal whether self-esteem is at the core of the problem. It can highlight things such as negative body language (drooping shoulders, downcast eyes, poor posture). We are also often unaware of our negative thoughts and the style of our conversation. Blaming the other (the world that won't give us a chance) reveals our innermost thoughts about our self.

A good life coach will help us connect with our natural enthusiasm and talent. Once this is realised and internalised, prospective employers sense it immediately. It's wonderful to see as a person emerges from the shell of their learned behaviour. When this happens, we become an irresistible force in anything we want to achieve.

In my case, for example, physical exercise alone was unsuccessful at healing back pain until I included affirmations and visualisations into the mix. The system only seems to function properly when action is taken on several levels.

Changing one's belief system is not as easy as some might suggest. There are people who will sell you products that claim to improve your self-image quickly, if you are gullible enough to buy them. You may be duped along the way; I know I have been. But I believe it is your duty to your self and to life to continue to evolve and strip away the learned and fearful behaviour of your past.

After my last session with the psychologist who treated me for anxiety, I believed there was little place for medication in the resolution of this frightening illness. This view was formed because of my own experience after a number of years of unsuccessful treatment with medication. Now, on reflection, and after listening to respected people in the medical, personal growth and spirituality fields, I have changed my view.

This change in my thinking came about because of the way I gradually overcame back pain. As I described earlier I used painkillers to assist me to confront and to defeat back pain. In the case of anxiety, the problem was that I never found a suitable, effective medication.

Almost by accident I was prescribed a new type of drug for the relief of back pain. This drug also happened to calm my anxiety. Even though it wasn't a cure, it saved me from having to take more than one type of medication, which in itself can be frustrating. This assisted me while I continued to develop and apply a new program I had set for myself.

I must say that the practice of meditation has had a profoundly beneficial effect on my anxiety. Without it I don't believe I would've survived, because I found that prescribed medication often left me with a sense of powerlessness.

Even though I believe that the practice of long-term meditation can ultimately defeat many anxiety disorders, I see no reason to suffer in the meantime. This is where prescription medicine has an important role to play in easing the immediate suffering and pain of anxiety.

Medication should be taken to assist you while you get your life in order. If you believe medication alone is the solution, then you will very likely not take *action* to confront your fears—and ultimately you will not experience true resolution and peace of mind. It's important to understand the clear difference between passively waiting to be cured, versus taking action and being part of the cure. If you take prescribed medicine and at the same time make changes to balance your life, that medication will be more successful.

I recall how I used to take my prescription medication with a certain amount of contempt. Looking back I'm sure that this attitude made it less effective for me. Remember, whatever the mind believes deeply will most certainly have a direct influence on the body. So, to manifest peace of mind from a position of anxiety one has to have the right intention and attitude when taking prescribed medication.

It's amazing how powerful the mind is when it comes to a treatment being successful or not. This has been clearly shown in double-blind trials when new drugs are tested. It's common for those receiving the placebo treatment to show great improvement, because in their mind, at a deep level, they believe that they're receiving the new drug.

At every level of life, all things are placebos. The amount of good or poor health we experience has to do with the degree to which we believe in particular things. I remember when I was taking powerful painkillers for back pain that they would sometimes work extremely well and at other times not at all. When I examined these situations I found that my level of fear at the time determined how effective the drug was. On other occasions, when I was in pain and chose not to take painkillers, I would get a similar result. It all depended on my outlook.

Sometimes I might be suffering badly, but without realising it I'd become engrossed in something I was doing. Minutes later I would notice my pain levels had dropped dramatically. I also found that when pain fluctuated at these times I was not necessarily having negative thoughts. These situations showed me how the subconscious mind was influencing the level of suffering or the feeling of wellbeing.

I eventually discovered that it is when one's mind is fully engrossed in the current moment that pain is reduced or disappears altogether. This is because the subconscious has less influence at times of high concentration. It takes a conscious effort to be fully in the moment. If you truly consider this statement, you will realise how often we are actually un-conscious.

I've found over time that the great spiritual teachers and leaders in the areas of metaphysics and business were indeed right. Whatever I've concentrated on, and have taken action on, has come true for me. If you concentrate on anything consistently, you will eventually bring it into your life. By concentrating on any pain you're experiencing you unfortunately only help it to grow stronger. If you concentrate on gratitude, more reasons for gratitude will come into your life.

When you look towards the good you will find it. As I came to understand that I was the creator who was manifesting my life experience, I also began to live my life with a reverence that I'd not practised before.

12

Satisfaction

SATISFACTION IS SOMETHING we all wish to achieve in our lives. We try hard to attain it in our day-to-day living. Our thoughts of satisfaction are also attached to goals. Inevitably, these goals are set somewhere in the future.

The future can be the next minute, the next day, five years from now or half a lifetime away. The thing I've noticed since I began meditation is that the pursuit of goals is something of an illusion. I don't mean the goals themselves. It's wonderful if you have (worthy) goals, because without them our lives would be aimless. It is the pursuit itself that is the problem.

When we push hard towards a goal our attention is often focused on the result. If we do this, we lose something—the ability to be here and now. Once the goal is set the thinking usually goes something like this: 'When I pass my exams I'll be alright. I'll get that better job and be able to buy a house and new car. If I increase my superannuation payments I'll be financially secure when I retire'.

The interesting thing about striving for goals is that often when we reach them they don't fulfil our expectations. The satisfaction we thought would be ours when we reach the goal is either not experienced, or if it is, it's only felt for a short time and then the feeling disappears. When this happens our *lack* of satisfaction deepens.

In the latter part of my fishing career, when I was having a particularly good run, the money I earned never gave me the satisfaction I had pictured. This was despite my earnings sometimes exceeding my expectations. My fear of poverty had grown to such a degree that it would have taken a much greater amount of money to experience satisfaction. A million dollars might have done it—but even this would've only been for a short while.

In contrast, my early fishing years gave me far more satisfaction, even though I earned a fraction of my later income. During this time I had general goals but the great difference was that my attention wasn't totally focused on the result. My satisfaction was much deeper because my mind was largely in the present. By being in the moment I was truly able to enjoy the natural beauty of my surroundings. I wasn't spending a large percentage of my time trying to predict my future. My satisfaction was profound because I really saw and felt the beautiful blueness of the ocean, and smelt that wonderful salty air with my whole being.

There is a great advantage in developing positive visualisations as far as satisfaction is concerned. It enables us to see and experience things from the perspective of the present moment, just as we would when we state an affirmation in the present tense. Visualisations develop our belief system, and it's the belief system that guides us to achieve—or to fail—depending on what we allow into our mind. Setting goals and regularly achieving them helps build our level of satisfaction in life.

The normal, worrying chatter of the mind is always drawing on the unsuccessful past and forecasting doom in the future. Even though this process (negative visualisation) can feel like a natural way of thinking for many of us, it is simply a destructive habit we've developed. Positive affirmations and visualisations set in the now are energy creating, whereas negative thoughts or pictures tend to deplete us.

Today, after several years of visualisation, I experience great joy and satisfaction when I ride my mountain bike near the river. I feel connected to my surroundings with a depth that is profound. It is exactly like the visualisations I created when I was an invalid in bed. I used to feel the texture of the air as I streamed down a hill. I would practise being amazed when I'd round a corner and see the turquoise colour of the river on the incoming tide. For me, there is no desensitising of the view, just an ever-growing appreciation for the beauty that surrounds me.

When I was financially prosperous with my lobster boat many of my thoughts were concerned with the next possible breakdown, the repayment of bank loans, and how I was performing compared to other skippers. It's clear to me now that my mind was anywhere but in the present.

You simply cannot have high levels of satisfaction in anything you do if your thoughts are mostly focused on negative issues in the past or in the future. Your relationships can't flourish if, in the middle of a conversation, you are thinking about your problems instead of giving your attention to the person you are talking to.

Not only does the other person feel this instinctively, but that same negative energy you are generating serves to depress your natural happiness. When you clear away all the fears, anxieties and concerns, you'll discover that happiness and satisfaction is truly your natural state of being.

I recall when I was quite young asking my father why he had to worry so much. His answer was, 'You'll find out when you get older'. He was exactly right. I *learnt* to become a worrier by my mid-twenties.

When one is driven by fear of poverty they are training to be the perfect student at the University of Fear. Yet, I have also learnt that if one can be taught to worry, one can also be taught to create a mind that experiences trust and optimism. A trusting mind tends to experience more satisfaction with life.

I'm not an expert at doing this yet but I am gaining more experience at it with the passing of time. Quite often now, when in the middle of mental turmoil, I'm able to stop and realise where my mind is taking me. Generally it's off to some future disaster where the predicted outcome has little basis in reality.

For example, when I'm dealing in the stock market and am about to buy some shares, my mind will often throw up a story about how this company could go bankrupt. I find it attempts to add truth to the movie it's playing by reminding me of past failures where I lost my total investment.

As soon as I become conscious of this I look to the successes in my portfolio to remind myself that I now know what I'm doing. This then confirms to me that I'm a much better investor than when I first began. I then bring myself back to the present moment and get on with it. I'm comforted knowing that I've done my homework and I can handle myself in the market in any situation.

To gain greater satisfaction from life we need to realise that we are not our thoughts. Our thoughts are just learned behaviours. As we come to a deeper understanding of this we also begin to take our thoughts less seriously. If, at the same time, we become aware that our mind is leading us off into the future or the past (attempting to maintain the status quo) we can smile to ourselves knowing that we are much more than our internal video of worries and fears.

As we become more conscious of these processes taking place, our fear will begin to recede. Joy starts to rise in us whether we're involved in the simplest task or in the act of realising a goal. The old saying, 'It's the journey that counts, not the destination', starts to become true. This is how satisfaction truly begins to grow in the different areas of life.

In the developed world we not only seem to be in a rush to get somewhere but that rush appears to be gathering momentum. Anxiously we feel we need the many new things that come onto the market, and if we don't have them, or can't afford them, we feel guilty and inadequate. Compounding this is the constant advertising we are exposed to. The problem with this is that it drives our fears of there *not being enough*. It also fosters feelings of inferiority because the advertising compares us to picture-perfect people. These are examples that nobody can realistically live up to. And I would add, who would want to, because true satisfaction cannot be found in things outside our self. It's an internal process that creates the feeling of satisfaction, in the same way that the emotions of joy, love or compassion are generated.

It's important to remember that we are always the creators of our satisfaction by the way we choose to process our life experiences. As our processing abilities improve we begin to accept ourselves for who we are and where we are right now. Coming to this realisation can relieve us of some very heavy burdens indeed. The net result is higher levels of satisfaction.

Criticising developed countries for their excesses is, I believe, a mistake, because in doing so we ignore the great advances made by those societies. The world would be poorer if not for the medical achievements that help so many, and the technology that has enabled, for example, the rapid evolution of global communication. Such criticism also ignores the fact that developed countries typically do not have substantial portions of their populations dying of starvation, as is often the case in developing countries. Developed nations on the whole have strong social welfare systems in place. They may not be perfect, but without them, life would be much more difficult for those who are not so fortunate.

One of the current side effects of living in a developed society is stress. As a result of this stress, people now are actually deriving less satisfaction from their lives than those in previous generations. This is because the seeking of satisfaction outside of one's self only perpetuates despair. I see nothing wrong with having or wanting material things but these desires must be kept in balance with the spiritual side of life. Material craving alone simply cannot fulfil us.

Like many in the west I have been guilty of viewing some eastern cultures and developing countries in particular as having little to offer or teach us. I didn't look beneath the surface. All I noticed was the poverty and the differences between us. Today I understand there is often great wisdom to be found in many of these cultures.

Do such cultures have the answers to life? Once again the explanation is a paradox. The answer is both yes and no. If we look at some of these societies whose cultures go back over 5000 years, we might ask why they are suffering today when their spiritual wisdom is so enlightened.

The suffering of these peoples is often a result of their history of abuse by ancient kingdoms and invading foreign powers, right through to modern-day dictators. The fact is that meditating or praying for much of one's time will not solve all of one's day-to-day problems. It takes action in the physical world to achieve that, but it also takes meditation and contemplation to keep that action in balance.

I do believe that those of us in the west can learn from these cultures. We may discover that it's our spiritual disconnection from life that causes the great hunger in us, which yearns to be filled. In the end it's only at the spiritual level that true and lasting peace and satisfaction will be found.

Since the industrial revolution, we have driven ourselves so hard to succeed and conquer the world that we have lost touch with our self. When I say this I mean who we really are, the self that is beyond body or mind. This concept of the self—as our spiritual heart, the essence of us—is at the core of all religions.

At different points in life we experience connections at this level. It might be when we feel a deep reverence in a natural setting. You may also have experienced it during a conversation with someone in which you both felt expanded and profoundly understood. It could have been a conversation in which compassion was extended to you and you were able to be yourself and truly accepted as that. Of course this would only happen if you were able to give the same gifts to the other person. At this point a spiritual connection (energy flow) would have taken place.

Once again it is a matter of creating balance if we want to have satisfaction in our lives. Taking time out each day from our busy schedules is vital. This time is separate from something you might choose to do for relaxation. Relaxation is sometimes viewed as a way of escaping from problems. This covers a range of different activities. But if those activities include things to help you forget your problems then they are not likely to be helping you.

The practice of meditation, walking in natural settings, or sitting by a lake, river or ocean will assist in bringing about the kind of calm peace I am talking about. I also consider reading books of wisdom to be a meditative practice. After this, when you take part in other activities for pleasure, you will enjoy them even more. If some of those activities were spiritually harmful to you, you may find after a while that they no longer interest you. The reason is that you will have become more conscious and are drawn to things that are more aligned with your higher good.

Changes are subtle and you are not likely to experience a new life overnight. From my own experience and from studying in this area, change is more a gentle realisation of what brings you happiness and joy. This change can sometimes occur quickly, but generally it's more likely to evolve over your lifetime.

Many of us go from birth to death never seeking the answers to life. This involves living predominantly in the material world and believing that there is nothing to life beyond the five senses. But if you are reading this book then, like me, you are interested in the meaning of life.

As you go about your journey you will feel more like an explorer than someone simply living an everyday existence. Hopefully you'll discover that there is more to life than you may have been taught growing up; and that this discovery has, at its core, the attributes of love, compassion and a deep understanding for all aspects of life.

You will realise your capacity to forgive is far greater than you thought possible. Some discover when they forgive others that they also experience a new sense of freedom. This freedom leads to peace of mind. Peace of mind also comes about when we understand that we have many more choices than we previously recognised.

We no longer have to make decisions from the narrow parameters of fear or from the perspective of the ego—because those things do not define who we are. Life does not restrict us to the limited beliefs of our upbringing. As we realise this we'll find that whatever situation we are faced with can be approached from different, new perspectives.

When my education ended after only two terms of first-year high school, I viewed myself as a labourer. I created this view from my environment, predominantly from my parents' experience of life. This belief stayed with me until my mid-forties. A change occurred when I started studying in the personal growth area. Bit by bit my picture of myself started to alter. This change wasn't easy. At first it was like extracting an infected tooth. But over time, as I tackled things I was afraid of, I discovered my fear would lessen in that area and very often it would disappear altogether.

After a few years of this I realised my view of my self had altered considerably. I began to feel like a writer, and an investor with a range of experience. A little later my view changed even further and I started to conceive that I could be a teacher and a speaker in the personal growth and spirituality field. It's interesting how, as my view changed, opportunities arrived to match my new belief system.

I think that the alterations I've made in my life since my marriage break-ups and my illnesses have changed me profoundly. I know that this is true because my picture of myself is now vastly different to the one I carried around for the first 40 years of my life. In fact, no matter how hard I try I can't see myself as a labourer anymore.

Forty years is a long time to carry around a self-image that keeps one restricted and ignorant to the endless possibilities that

life has to offer. We are limited by time in this physical body and because of that it is our duty to discover the truth about life as early as possible. Being the creators of our experience we need to make sure that our life is the one we intend for ourselves—a conscious creation. So, if you are looking to blame someone else for your situation, all that will guarantee is that you will remain stuck right where you are. Yes, there are some awful things that happen to us, but it is our response alone to those things that will determine our level of satisfaction in life.

Many ancient cultures clearly didn't have all the answers, but certainly I believe in a spiritual sense some of them did. Hindu and Buddhist cultures have existed for millennia. I recently watched a television program on the current state of Australian society. It talked about an inner emptiness that existed, one that we unsuccessfully try to satisfy with material things. Yet when the journalists travelled to India they discovered a different feel within that society. Yes, there was poverty but families had a close bond—a spiritual connection. It may be argued that this is all that is needed in life. However, though spiritual values are still practised today the populations of some of these countries continue to suffer high levels of poverty. This indicates that a purely spiritual outlook cannot solve all problems.

We in the west are so very good at taking action, and yet in the process of that furious endeavour we tend to overlook the divine. We miss the reverence in each precious breath we take and the joy of each new dawn, because we are moving too fast, like the mouse on the wheel.

When we realise individually that we have gifts to offer each other, gifts that cannot be measured strictly in financial terms, then we will grow in appreciation for life and for others. This appreciation will ultimately bring us an inner feeling of satisfaction.

13

Belief

EVERYTHING I HAVE read and experienced on the subject of belief shows me that it is our thoughts, and our depth of belief in those thoughts, which is the creating force in our life. This means, everything we experience until we die. Napoleon Bonaparte said, 'Imagination rules the world'. He is only one of many through millennia to believe that the power to create our own lives lies first in our thoughts and imagination, and secondly in the action that flows from that imagination. This carries even greater weight when we consider it in the context of having free will.

At first this philosophy was hard for me to accept. My adult life had taught me that I didn't have a choice in many of the things that happened to me, such as how other people treated me, accidents that occurred seemingly out of the blue, and the suffering that can befall any of us during our lifetime. Because of my upbringing I had a belief that it was always forces outside of me that controlled my destiny. School and society reinforced this belief.

Contrasting this was my experience in the very early years of my life. Up until about the age of nine I believed anything was possible. Now, as I'm approaching my mid-fifties I clearly understand that the outlook of the child—the one of limitless possibilities—is the very essence of life itself.

I recall in primary school how we were taught that the authorities of earlier centuries believed the world to be flat. The vast lands of the Americas and Australia were left undiscovered for centuries, not because sailing ships were incapable of making the journey, but because of the beliefs held at the time.

One doesn't have to look back very far historically to see navigation maps with drawings of terrifying sea serpents and warnings of horrible outcomes if explorers ventured too far. Illustrations of ships falling off the edge of the world abounded. Like the sailors of old, we as individuals are always fighting serpents because entrenched beliefs can make them seem so real.

As suggested earlier we should always challenge our beliefs, on any matter. We need to do this because these beliefs may be founded on incorrect information. Of course, the ego won't like you doing this because it sees its role as maintaining the status quo. The reason that change is so difficult for most of us is because of the ego. The ego is the governor of your personality—the self-image. It forms this image from information gathered during your life and from your life's experience. Anything outside of its knowledge is unknown and therefore frightening—in other words, the terrifying edge of a flat world.

Questioning one's beliefs will at first bring up resistance, often in the form of fear, anger or denial. If we take the advice of the ego we will shrink back to the familiar and the safe. Each time we do this, a little more of our true self dies as our view of the world shrinks. The ego will always keep us restricted, like an overly protective mother attempting to shield us from the big bad world.

By continually questioning our beliefs and asking where they came from, we will find that often they're the beliefs of others that we've picked up environmentally. We may discover that the *reality* of what we believed about something might not only be different from our belief, but that it could have a number of probable outcomes. Rather than this being a frightening revelation, it can actually give us a sense of freedom. This freedom comes about because we realise we suddenly have more choices in any situation.

Each day I find I still have to question my beliefs. There is a lot of resistance from my ego at times because, like most people, I would rather avoid change than go through it. But if we look into our hearts and see our avoidance, we will learn that we are missing the chance to grow and become more than we currently are.

Now I am able to recognise this resistance when it's occurring. Because I'm more conscious in this area than I was before my personal growth work, I can see things from different perspectives. This helps me reach decisions more quickly and to take appropriate action.

There are still some occasions when I find myself dealing with an old fear and that fear might bog me down in procrastination. When this is the case life usually creates a situation where I'm forced to take action. In hindsight I often find that I've expended more energy procrastinating than if I'd taken action in the first place. Remember, any action we may take, even if it turns out to be wrong, is still beneficial because it moves us forward and out of procrastination. Some people live their entire lives in procrastination, which is simply a life lived in fear.

Sometimes when I'm being cautious about a situation, I ask myself whether or not I'm making my decision out of fear or trust. I never answer the question intellectually, because the mind tends to tell one stories in order to justify the ego's view of the situation. It's too easy to be caught up in the process of the thinking mind. I find the surest way is to go by feeling. After I've asked myself the question, it's my gut feeling that gives me the truest answer. As you become more conscious you will find that your gut feeling is accurate and will never let you down.

Evaluating fear this way is an extremely reliable method. In the end the choice is simple; you are either making a decision out of love or out of fear. Many of us don't realise that it's this simple—there really are no in-betweens. Love reflects trust and the sense that things will work out; fear always concentrates on what might go wrong.

The person who cheats on their income tax does so because of belief. If they asked themselves why they were not declaring all of their income, many would answer by claiming the system is unfair. Usually this is a superficial answer provided by the ego. Often at a deeper level they don't believe that they have the ability to earn enough money to live well and pay their taxes.

To consider these questions at the level of wisdom one has simply to go beyond the ego and ask the question honestly (whether it is about tax evasion or anything else). When you're making a choice because of fear, you will actually feel that fear in your gut. It's then that you have your answer. But if you truly believe you are justified in what you're doing at the level of wisdom, then there will be clarity in the answer that comes back. Your stomach will be settled and your mind will be free and clear.

If you ask any question of yourself with honesty in your heart, your instinct will not lie to you. Before you put this into practice you need to have gained some level of consciousness through a spiritual practice; otherwise your mind may deceive you.

Our body is always affected by what our mind believes. One day in my second year of fishing my father invited a fellow fisherman over for dinner. Our guest explained that his two sons had come to stay with him from the city because of the school holidays. He asked if it would be all right if he brought them along to dinner. My father said that would be fine. Knowing we were having marinated octopus for entrée the friend explained that his sons disliked octopus and asked if it would be okay if they just had the main course of pasta.

My father always prepared a very good dish of octopus and took pride in his ability to do so. Previously he'd experienced some people being squeamish about the dish—all those slimy tentacles and suction pads. The look alone was enough to turn some off the delicacy before they even tried it. This was back in the mid-sixties when the Australian palate wasn't very sophisticated in terms of world cuisine.

That evening when the guests arrived one of the boys immediately said, 'Did Dad tell you that we don't eat octopus because it makes us sick?' My father acknowledged that he was aware of this. He told the boys that we were having the octopus, but they were having something else. At first they were a little suspicious, but their fears were put to rest when my father showed them that he was cooking a special entree for them. When they discovered it was deep-fried prawns they were quite excited. Apparently this was one of the few types of seafood they liked.

The evening went particularly well. Those of us who ate the octopus enjoyed it for its wonderful southern Italian flavours: the garlic, olive oil, parsley and vinegar. Everyone seemed to like the pasta, and the simple red wine was a perfect complement. I was 16 at the time and on this occasion Dad allowed me to have a small amount of wine with my meal, so this night I was feeling just like one of the men. Our two young guests were most animated about their entrée—they loved it.

'These are the best prawns we've ever tasted', the older boy said. The younger one agreed with an enthusiastic smile.

Some four hours later our evening drew to a close. As lobster fisherman we were usually in bed by ten because of our pre-dawn starts. Just as our guests were leaving, my father said to the boys that he hoped they'd enjoyed their octopus. They both looked at him with a quizzical expression.

At this point their father gave a knowing smile, for he understood what was about to happen. I think he went along with my father because he thought his sons had been babied a little in their upbringing.

'What octopus?' the younger one asked.

My father explained that they had actually eaten deep-fried octopus. He said he'd stripped the skin and suction pads off the tentacles, then cut them into lengths similar to king prawns. After this he put a few cuts in one end of each section and fanned it out like the tail of a prawn. The final concealment had been when he dipped them in batter and deep-fried them.

By this stage the colour had drained from the boys' faces. A few minutes later their appearance had taken on a somewhat blue-green colour. It was about then that they rushed past me and began vomiting on the front lawn.

Of course they were too sick to protest very much at the time. When they recovered a short while later, my father asked them why they didn't get sick when they ate the octopus, as they normally would have. But the boys didn't answer this question. Their only response was, 'You know that octopus makes us sick'.

This story shows clearly how our beliefs (the ego) have a direct effect on our body. Not only did the boys not get sick when they ate the octopus, but they actually enjoyed it so much that they claimed, 'These are the best prawns we've ever tasted'. While they believed this to be true they were not sick for a period of up to four hours. That was their reality. Only when this belief was shattered did the ego come into play. It very quickly established its own belief system (the status quo) for the boys concerning octopus. The result was that they then had to be sick.

At the age of eight I first went out on a lobster boat for the day. I remember it well because I felt seasick the whole time. My father and his skipper told me that if I continued to go out over a period of a few days that I would get over it. The reality was that I never did. My seasickness continued, even over a lobster career that spanned more than 20 years on the ocean.

I mainly felt ill when I left the fresh air of the open deck and went into the cabin. The stale air mixed with the smell of engine fumes usually had me feeling unsettled in the stomach within 20 minutes. This situation was made worse by the fish bait we always carried.

If I had to check the radar or steer a compass course, that was enough to make me want to throw up. This feeling only eased off when I'd go outside into the fresh air again. It never completely left me until I was back on dry land. I experienced the same feeling of sickness if I attempted to read whilst travelling on most modes of transport, although I was okay on large planes.

Interestingly my mother recounts a story of when I was three years old. It was at the time when my father was crewing on my uncle's boat. My uncle decided to leave Lancelin Bay and head to Fremantle, which was approximately nine hours' travelling time on his boat. On board were my uncle, his wife, my father and mother, my sister Nancy and I; there were also our three cousins. All of us children were under eight years of age.

Unfortunately the sea-breeze came in much earlier than my uncle expected. This meant the voyage took almost 12 hours in rough conditions. Apparently all the women and children were quite ill, except for me. Mum tells me that I enjoyed every minute of the journey, and not only that—I sang most of the way. Even today, more than 50 years later, she can't get over how I thrived in those conditions. Apparently it was a great adventure to me.

I've no doubt that because I was very young, I'd taken on at some level the responses of those who were suffering around me, and that this conditioned me for my later seasickness. I also recall hearing stories growing up of seasickness and airsickness from my mother and father, when they recounted their own experiences and those of others.

A child's brain is constantly soaking up information, which is fed into its belief system. Whether that information is correct or not, it has no way of knowing. Two children exposed to the same information over the short term may have different beliefs resulting from that data. But if they are continually given the same information about certain things (by the family, the environment) then there is a much higher probability that this view will form part of their belief system.

The medical solution for my motion sickness was to take anti-nausea tablets. On the surface this sounded fine, but in reality the medication left me feeling drowsy, which wasn't ideal when one was skippering a lobster boat and operating machinery.

During my earlier years of learning about metaphysics I saw an explanation that said seasickness or motion sickness comes from not feeling safe in the world. In other words it is a fear. In my fishing days I would have said, 'What a load of rubbish—I love the ocean!'

When I began meditation I learnt that it was an effective way to dissolve accumulated stress (fear). I took up the practice mainly to overcome back pain and anxiety. To my surprise, after two years of meditating I found my seasickness had reduced considerably. A year later it had vanished altogether. Today, I can read a book in a car, bus or boat without the slightest feeling of motion sickness.

I can't imagine any other treatment that could have healed this problem in such a natural way. It's clear that meditation has had a profound effect on my life. It generates in me a deep feeling of peace and comfort—a place of sanctuary.

There are so many beliefs we have as individuals that are simply not true. It's through our beliefs that we either struggle against the difficulties of life, or we move forward with much less resistance. A high level of resistance means that when problems arise, we try to get life to change so as to fit our view. We waste enormous energy in this area and can't understand why life is doing this to us.

The fact is that problems are simply part of life. However, these problems bring us constant opportunities to learn and grow in the process of overcoming them. If we stop blaming life for treating us badly and apply that same energy to finding a solution to our problems (when we look a solution is always found) we will move forward with much less resistance.

I believe one of the reasons I suffered so badly for so many years with my back was simply because of my belief of who I was. It's clear to me now that life created this situation so I might come to understand that I was much more than a labourer. Even though I enjoyed many aspects of that life, in my heart I secretly wanted to be intellectual, and a success in business. The problem was the information stored in my brain during my upbringing only allowed my ego to see me as a labourer.

When I injured my back I was shattered. It took many years for me to reduce my pain. For a long time I was trying to go back to being a labourer, yet life was trying to tell me to do otherwise. Time and time again it showed me through teachers and job offers that I could be so much more. But my ego kept me trapped, and fed me stories of pity. It told me about how I wasn't qualified for anything else, and how I would never be.

Today, the things I'm involved in are a far cry from the labouring work I once did. I'm actually immersed in a number of areas I could only have dreamt about in my earlier life. When I look back and see how great the change has been, it's understandable why it took so long, and why it was so painful.

Our brains are just like computers: if we install new programs (affirmations) and believe that new information, we begin to perform differently. We can shape and mould ourselves any way we want. The problem is that unless we realise it is our mind that achieves this for us, we will simply be at the mercy of the stored beliefs from our childhood. That would be fine, if we all had the perfect upbringing, but unfortunately that's simply not the case for many of us.

Becoming aware of how the mind works and gaining control of its functioning is the key to creating a new belief system. After we gather the new information that we want and begin to apply it, the brain then starts to act on that material. Over time this new information influences our thinking, and in turn, our behaviour.

The old thought patterns don't disappear completely. It's more a case of them being overridden by the new information. Now and again some old fears will resurface, but you will have the foundational strength of your new beliefs. As you reaffirm the new information, the old fears will once again fade into the background.

For many years I unquestioningly accepted the information given to me by medical and other professionals. This was one of the reasons I was unable to ride a bicycle for all those years. Whenever I attempted to ride a bike, and experienced back pain, it would remind me of the disc protruding in my spine. I accepted this until I received new information. I then decided to create a new belief about having a healthy back and being able to ride a bike with complete comfort and ease.

Healing my neck pain was significant because it came at a time when the pain had reached its highest intensity. Even though I started with an affirmation from Louise Hay's book *You Can Heal Your Life,* I don't believe that alone would have healed me. I believe what healed me was more that I considered deeply the causes suggested in the book.

Words like stubbornness and inflexibility certainly struck a chord with me. If they hadn't I'm sure I'd still be suffering neck pain today. It's interesting that many people suffer from neck pain. This indicates to me that a lot of us are stubborn and inflexible in our approach to certain issues. As with all of us these traits simply come from beliefs, and they in turn come from incorrect information.

When you believe you are right and another person, or the world, is wrong, then you may be investing too much in your position. This attitude can build resistance to the flow of life. The fact is there are many ways of doing things and seeing things. If we can let go of our position for a moment and realise this, our view suddenly expands. At this very point we gain understanding and wisdom. Once we reach this stage, compassion automatically flows.

I began to understand one doesn't need to force their beliefs onto others, and that it's okay, even interesting, to listen to other views. If you can do that you begin to generate a frequency of respect. Because you are dealing with energy here, other like energy will synchronise with your own. This may not happen right away but at some point it certainly will. Just suspend your expectations and trust that it will happen. When you synchronise with other positive energy your mood will lift and also your physical energy levels will increase.

Another important milestone for me was when I stopped trying to force life to fit my plans. After I aligned myself more with the flow, rather than trying to swim against the current, my neck pain backed off considerably. So once again beliefs were at the core of my neck pain, just as they are with most pain. Discomfort is always a result of beliefs that are restrictive or negative. A negative outlook causes tension in the body. When this tension is unrelenting in intensity or duration, it develops into pain and illness.

Having a positive outlook creates spiritual growth as well as physical and mental good health. The person who has good health, successful relationships, and general prosperity doesn't achieve this through luck. They tend to take the approach that there is a solution to each situation that arises. Fundamentally they are always looking to the good in life, rather than the bad. These people are generally happy to pass on their knowledge and experience to others, and to assist them in achieving their dreams.

When I was young, I thought people who were affluent weren't stressed by problems because of their financial ability to solve those problems. It was only when I was in my forties that I began to notice that these people rarely solved problems by throwing money at them. Once again, above all things, their success stemmed from their belief that no matter what the situation was, there would be a way to solve it.

Because people with this mindset believe this, they are usually rewarded with a solution. When one takes this approach with the difficulties of life, positive energy frequencies will always connect to assist you. But remember, this has to be a deeply held mindset. You can't expect to be successful in any area if your mind is dominated by thoughts of fear and failure.

This energy ('life' or 'God') is interactive, and it comes to you directly via your mind (free will). If you don't gain control over your mind, you'll be much like a car travelling down the street without a driver at the wheel. By becoming the driver of your mind you can go on an adventure through this experience called life.

Believe deeply, take action, and watch things begin to match your innermost thoughts.

14

The Way Ahead

EVERY NOW AND then I find I have to stop myself striving for enlightenment. I do this when I realise I'm working too hard to reach a goal or trying too hard to gain peace of mind. Fundamentally, I know enlightenment is not out there. One only has to go inside to find the answers. You might ask: 'If it's so easy why isn't everyone practising this "going inside" business, and what of those who go inside all the time and still suffer?'

This came up in conversation with a friend the other day who said he often locks himself away and immerses himself in spiritual reading. He finds when he does this for long periods he begins to feel depressed. This is because we are part of the whole and not separate from the rest of life.

A person who is totally immersed in spirituality is in many ways just as badly off as someone who lives completely in the material world. I suggested to my friend that at such times he seek out human company. Even if he had no-one to make contact with, a walk by the river would increase his energy and in turn lift his spirits.

Going to the local shopping centre will also help connect you to the energy generated by others. You may not speak to anyone but the energy there will permeate your system and give you a lift. There is always some positive action you can take, however small.

If you're busy in the material world, meditation is a wonderful tool for slowing down the frenetic pace of modern life. As I've mentioned before, sitting silently for 30 minutes, particularly in a natural, or quiet, setting, will achieve a similar result. When this is practised you may begin to feel something very powerful. It's at these times you will realise that you are part of the whole of life—not a separate entity, but an integral component of something vast.

When you experience moments like these you will begin to slow down your anxious striving, whether it be material or spiritual, because you will realise you are already there. You just have to pause for contemplation each day and begin to enjoy the view of life.

What I'm suggesting is not just an intellectual process; it truly is a spiritual connection. When practised twice a day, once before breakfast and again in the late afternoon, you may be surprised at the calmness and peace that starts to come into your life.

Don't expect miracles right away—it may take six months or so before you even notice changes taking place. I think the key to success here will always be some sort of regular practice to give yourself an increasing level of tranquillity.

One thing that has always struck me from my observations of Buddhist monks and long-term meditators is the calmness that emanates from them. Often they are happy people with a good sense of humour. The Dalai Lama is a wonderful example of this. When you listen to or spend time with people like this, you can actually feel something peaceful and compassionate coming from them. Once again, what you are experiencing is occurring at the level of energy.

After approximately ten years of meditation I have gained a glimpse into this world of the spiritual. I'm far from an expert in this area but many times I've experienced its wonderful calmness. I certainly have no desire to become a monk, but I have a deep appreciation for the positive and uplifting effect of this type of practice.

There are few people in the world who are in an enlightened state all of the time. But I believe that there is a growing number of the world's population expanding in spiritual awareness. The solution to the world's problems will eventually come from this spiritual perspective. This means that once we have gained a higher level of spiritual consciousness, we will start to live our lives from the spiritual viewpoint. This is a view that we can apply in a practical way in the real world—in our everyday lives.

As long as a small percentage of countries command much of the world's wealth, animosity is bound to exist among those who have little. This situation is not necessarily the fault of developed countries. But when wealthy nations start to extend compassion and provide genuine programs of development to less fortunate nations, greater peace will be the result. Developing countries will then gain access to world markets and at the same time the world will have access to their markets. Remember, these are markets that would never previously have existed.

The fundamental law of life is *growth*. If it is kept in balance, personal growth leads to spiritual growth, which then flows on to creativity and prosperity of the individual. On an energy level this is contagious; it can quickly transmit to entire nations, if encouraged.

When all people prosper, the breeding grounds of hatred are diminished. Of course this improved material prosperity cannot last unless it goes hand in hand with genuine compassion for our fellow human beings. This is not just because we should have compassion for economic or humanitarian reasons, but because we finally understand that we are all one living entity.

Ignoring parts of the world that are suffering is akin to going out into freezing weather with only one boot on. If we continue that way for very long we will eventually lose our exposed foot to frostbite. As a result, the whole body will suffer.

This is why there is currently so much turmoil in the world. Too many parts of the world (the whole) believe they are separate. As long as they believe this and act against the interests of the whole, the suffering in the world will continue. If wealthy countries try to ignore and isolate themselves from the suffering many, it will mean a continuation of world suffering.

I am saddened by current events, and yet heartened at the same time. My sadness is for the distress of many, which seems unnecessary, particularly when we have the capacity, but not the will, to end that distress. Even though there is a great deal of violence in the world at the moment, I feel it is drawing to a conclusion, perhaps moving towards something that has been foretold since the dawn of time.

This may be the completion of the infantile and juvenile age of human kind, leading us into adulthood, and then into the final stage of enlightenment: wisdom. Beyond that I can only speculate, but I know from things I have experienced and read about, that it will be something extraordinarily wonderful—like the presence one experiences in a profound meditation: something warm, supportive, and loving, and at the same time powerful.

Before humanity reaches the point of wisdom it really is up to us to play our part as individuals. The flow of positive energy has to gain momentum before we can move to the point of wisdom. If we wait for governments to make the world a better place, we may be disappointed. For energy to arrive at the point of change it takes an alignment of power. That power comes from us, as individuals. Just as someone else can't change our life, no matter how hard they try, unless we make the decision to do so, the world cannot go forward until there is an overwhelming choice to heal on the individual level.

Because each of us is truly a crucial and fundamental part of something vast, it will take our individual effort to build this positive energy up to the point of change. Of course none of this will take place unless we want to become conscious in the first place. We could choose to sit and watch television for 40 hours a week. Possibly we are like the many people who dream only of retirement, thinking that life will be better then.

By developing a spiritual practice you can be in touch with this energy, which will always guide you in the right direction. I can't promise you that every day will be positive, because life simply doesn't work that way. By getting in touch with this energy you will become more effective in working towards your dreams and goals. When this is applied at the individual level in great enough numbers, then the world will experience positive change. So rather than wait for something cosmic to happen, we can begin by working on ourselves right now.

There is a sound reason for personal and spiritual growth, because as one grows, fears shrink proportionally, and a wider view of life is gained. It's this lessening of fear at the global level that advances humankind and draws us closer to wisdom.

When the flow of energy is not going in your direction and things are not fitting in with your plans, you will learn to wait until the tide turns again. I came to understand this lesson by being involved in the stock market. I now sit quietly and patiently until the opportunities present themselves rather than trying to make them happen. Because of this approach I'm more peaceful within myself as an investor rather than being a nervous trader pouncing on every half-opportunity.

If we force things, it usually means we are coming from a place of fear. I haven't overcome all of my fears, but I can say that I have fewer fears today than five years ago, and many less than a decade earlier. When I look back on the fears I've conquered, I'm surprised that I never confronted them earlier. It's only after we've conquered a fear that we realise it was never as bad as we imagined. And that's the secret. Confront your fears step by step, one at a time. Avoiding a fear or running from it only encourages it to grow larger in our minds. When you confront a fear you will see it dissipate, like an ocean mirage in the face of a cooling sea breeze.

You may think that my recommendation to develop a spiritual practice might not fit in with our high-paced, modern life. It may even seem like a waste of time. Ten years ago I would have agreed with you. But now I know if I hadn't taken this spiritual road, it's unlikely that I would have overcome chronic neck and sciatic pain.

For over 20 years I tried much of what mainstream and alternative medicine had to offer, including surgery. In the end these things were unsuccessful. In fact, I might still be investigating those same treatments if I hadn't been told in clear terms that there was nothing else that could be done for me.

Our thinking, and therefore our processing of life, is the cause of many different illnesses in our bodies. A lot of us are like mice running inside a wheel. Initially it seems as though we are getting somewhere fast. It's only when we stop that we realise the destination is not quite what we thought it was. If we don't take essential time-out for ourselves, as well as enjoy the journey along the way, we are likely to experience increasing health problems. By not taking this time-out we will also experience something else—a deepening sense of lack in our lives.

The drive for material things and the rapid pace of society can build up stress in any of us. One of the side effects of this is an increasing crime rate. Currently this appears to be accentuated by the difference between the haves and the have-nots. The truth is, crime has its basis in feelings of separateness. If we look a little deeper we'll find it is a spiritual separateness. When we haven't come to know our true self there will always be a sense of aloneness. Someone who is committing a crime would not be doing so if they'd arrived at the universal truth that we are all one.

This understanding is realised when one person kills another. At the time when the physical act takes place, the belief system will justify the outcome. Not long after, the heart tells us that something is inherently wrong. This is why soldiers retaliating against a brutal enemy become crushed in spirit the longer they go on killing—even if their cause is in the name of freedom.

Because we are intrinsically one entity (one great interactive energy field) everything is utterly connected in every way. When we do harm, it comes back to us on some level. It's exactly the same if we apply ourselves to do good; it will benefit us sooner or later.

In the energy field, thoughts are very powerful and they eventually manifest physically in some way. This is especially so if a particular thought dominates our thinking. So unless we use our minds intelligently we can do harm in the same way as if we were to take physical action.

The thing to understand is that anything created (by thought or physical action) is always transmitted back to us in some way. This is simply because like energies harmonise with one another. A person who harbours bitterness and distrust will always experience these things in their life. On the other hand, one who practises understanding and compassion, and sees the humour in life, tends to encounter those things.

I don't want you to become paranoid about what you're thinking all the time, rather, to become aware of how you're using your mind. When you do this, the result is a more conscious approach to life.

The purpose of personal growth is to take in the spiritual, educational, relational and financial aspects of life. Not only are these fundamental to individual change, but also to an evolving world.

Dr John Sarno's philosophy on back injuries back up my experience that our thoughts affect our body. Sarno proposes that back injuries also lodge themselves in the consciousness of populations. His argument is that this is demonstrated by the explosion of back surgery that was taking place in the eighties and nineties. This is despite developed countries being less involved in physical labour than earlier generations. I would say that these emotional issues (beliefs) are transmitted at the level of energy across those populations. If we are unconscious we can easily be affected by the view of others.

I remember when I was a young man lobster fishing how we used to envy friends who had desk jobs because they didn't suffer from back pain like manual workers did. Yet today, office workers appear to be just as badly off. In fact, sedentary work can be just as deadly for the back, according to authority figures.

Sarno's view in some ways ties in with the metaphysical view. This is that lower back pain is caused by feeling (emotional) unsupported by life. Metaphysically, this injury pervading developed nations highlights their quest for the material. Often, the harder we pursue the material, the further we move away from our spiritual core. And because of this we feel less supported by life than we otherwise might.

I followed all the expert advice when I suffered back pain. An ergonomic expert even came out and evaluated my home-living situation. She recommended that I cut down the height of my brand new desk and buy a certain type of chair. I did this, but in the end it was all to no avail. It wasn't long after that I had back surgery, which unfortunately left me with even worse pain.

Years later when I challenged this pain at the movies using John Sarno's theory, I began to make progress. There I was doing the very thing I was told to avoid because it would cause me greater damage. Even though it was very difficult, I took the attitude that I was battling a belief, rather than a disc protrusion.

To feel my pain retreat that day, the way it did, encouraged me greatly. I thought, how could all those experts be so mistaken? The answer is because those experts had narrowed their views and locked in their beliefs. There are certainly cases that require back surgery, but I believe not to the extent that has occurred in the past. The fact that surgery in this area has currently declined says something about the outcomes that were being achieved.

I believe it's unfair of us to expect the medical fraternity and alternative medicine practitioners to solve all of our health problems. Good health has much more to do with taking responsibility for ourselves in life. You might take note of those who rarely fall ill. Yes, some may have good genetics, but from what I've observed, it's more their attitude and willingness to embrace life that is the key to their good health.

Before we ever get ill we need to ensure that the type of action we take in our daily lives gives us balance and happiness. In the end this approach is far more powerful in achieving good health than we might understand. Expecting a drug, a surgeon, or a herb to cure problems that have their origins in the dis-ease in one's life, is to deceive ourselves.

Happiness has its beginning in the mind—not only the experience of it but also its very creation. As more studies are done it is becoming clear that we truly are responsible for whether or not we experience a happy life.

It's not what is out there that determines happiness. I watched a young man on a current affairs program one night. He was born with an incomplete spinal cord. The result was that he had been left with deformed legs that were never going to develop properly. When he was younger, a surgeon had recommended to his parents that his legs be amputated because he said they would only hinder his mobility as he grew.

As I watched the story I discovered that here was a young man with a wonderful enthusiasm for life. He played wheelchair basketball. In one game I saw him in a collision that resulted in him landing on the floor. With great eagerness he righted his chair and installed himself into the driving position again, and then he quickly returned to the fray, as if he hadn't been inconvenienced at all.

When I listened to him being interviewed it was clear his approach to life was similar to his approach to sport. He did what made him happy and he applied himself with enthusiasm. I saw no trace of him dwelling on what he didn't have or couldn't do. He was entering college and had recently been dating a girl.

One scene that particularly inspired me was a video of when he was a child attending kindergarten. There were two rows of children dancing to music. In between these rows on the floor there he was, with something like an oversized bottle cap fitted to the base of his body. He was spinning around to the music by pushing himself with his hands. The thing that impressed me most was the look of wonder on his face. It was that of a person fully immersed in the joy of the moment.

When we can come to this point ourselves and not be influenced by fears of things past, and stop prophesying that the future might be even worse, *then* we will begin living in this moment.

The most joy, the most peace and gratitude, can only be found here and now. As we begin to immerse ourselves less in the past and focus more on this very moment, we really do start to banish our fears. By doing this we take a hand in shaping the quality of our life. Like a ship with a fully functional rudder, we can set our course and go with the current of life, and see where it takes us.

www.ingramcontent.com/pod-product-compliance
Ingram Content Group UK Ltd.
Pitfield, Milton Keynes, MK11 3LW, UK
UKHW020143250726
13967UKWH00002B/827

9 781425 112790